Some Christian books are written by ivory-tower theologians who seemingly have little connection to the painful struggles of life in a broken world. Other books are written by practitioners, but they sometimes lack biblical and theological fidelity. I am thrilled to endorse this work by Constable and McConnell. They get the theology of addiction right, but they also have ministered for many years in the trenches with addicts. They offer real help, not just pious platitudes. This book is the new gold standard for Christians and local churches who want to better understand addiction and more importantly, how to help addicts find victory through Christ.

Timothy K. Beougher
Professor of Evangelism and Church Growth, Southern Baptist Theological Seminary, Louisville, Kentucky

Addiction and the Local Church was a wonderful and tough read simultaneously. Wonderful as it's informative, theologically accurate and is written from a heart of love by the authors. Tough, because it's raw, blunt and honest, about sin, about addiction, about the confusion by the world to treat it and in the Church to rightly apply the gospel. The strength of this book is found in its deep love of Christ, the gospel and discipleship, but perhaps its greatest strength is it's understandably! We live in contradictory world, social media and A.I mean we can google just about anything and feel like an expert, while academia and especially theological academics tend to write books so abstract its hard from anyone to grasp, let alone apply the concepts being written about.

Addiction and the Local Church is written to the Local Church and for the local Christian. You will be able to understand the subject matter and apply the principles from God's Word. Mez and Andy are not salesmen, they are clients of the Word of God and they are truly under-shepherds of

Christ who love those to whom Christ has sent them to serve. This is a book I recommend you not only read, but study, share and apply in your life as a Christian disciple, called and commissioned to disciple others in the ways of Christ and His Word!

Stephen Bray
Lead Elder, Calvary Baptist Church,St. John's, Newfoundland;
Executive Director of Mile One Mission.

I know of few people who would be better qualified to write this book than my friends Andy Constable and Mez McConnell, for I know of few people who have been more committed to loving, caring for, and ministering to people with addictions. This book is not written by professors or clinicians but by pastors whose calling is to minister to broken people in hard places. May the Lord use it to equip many more Christians to better understand and better love those who struggle with addictions.

Tim Challies
Blogger and author

So often churches and pastors avoid addicts because they either lack a heart for them or simply have no idea what to do with them. The book you hold in your hands will be a great help for both. *Addiction and the Local Church* is an overdue and needed resource that will guide you on both the care of those struggling with addiction, as well as show you the value of these precious and hurting souls in desperate need of hope. The authors are both faithful pastors and skilled practitioners who offer timeless wisdom out of their own experiences that will serve pastors, church leaders, and caregivers alike. And all who read this will also be freshly reminded of the power of the gospel and the miracle it is for any of us to find forgiveness and salvation. Everyone should read this.

Brian Croft
Executive Director, Practical Shepherding

Addiction and the Local Church is a theologically robust, practical read. With real honesty and gospel hope, Constable and McConnell offer practical insights rooted in Scripture, making this an essential resource for any church serious about gospel-centered, transformative care.

Sharon Dickens
Director of Women's Ministry, 20Schemes

Andy and Mez serve up a timely reminder that it takes a church to care for those trapped in addiction. Through a combination of biblical clarity and raw frontline experience, they counsel us on how to love, disciple, and persevere with those who struggle. This book will stretch your theology, stir your compassion, and strengthen your church's mission.

Liam Garvie
Associate Pastor at Charlotte Chapel, Edinburgh;
International Director, Pillar Network

Addictions are everywhere – they existed in the rural area in which I mainly grew up and they exist in the post-industrial Northern town that I now live in. Wherever there are Christian churches, you will almost certainly find people with addictions. The big problem is, lots of us don't have a clue what to do for people who struggle with them.

That is why I am so pleased to have this book. Andy and Mez carefully help us think through what addictions are, how they operate and what Christian churches can uniquely do to help those facing addictions to become faithful men and women of God. Drawing upon their experiences discipling dozens of people from addicted background, they have given us a fantastic tool to not only think through the nature of addictions, but to truly help those from addicted backgrounds as they come into contact with our churches.

Stephen Kneale
Pastor, Oldham Bethel Church, Oldham

This book shows there is real hope for all addicts. It shows the Bible understands the problem. Jesus has the power, but there is a cost for church. If you look at addicts and feel you don't know what to do. Read this book.

Steve Levy
Lead Pastor, Mount Pleasant Baptist Church, Swansea

Addiction and the Local Church explores the biblical foundations for understanding addiction and offers practical guidance for churches seeking to reach, disciple, and care for those struggling with substance abuse. Drawing on theological insight and personal experience, Andy Constable and Mez McConnell offer a guide to gospel-centered ministry that tackles the sin and suffering inherent in addiction. For churches working to bring Christ's transformative power to broken communities, this book is a vital resource.

Mario Maneville
Lead Pastor, Reformed Faith Mission Community Church, Cape Town, South Africa

ADDICTION AND THE **LOCAL CHURCH**

ANDY CONSTABLE & **MEZ MCCONNELL**

CHRISTIAN FOCUS

print ISBN 978-1-5271-1300-8

ebook ISBN 978-1-5271-1389-3

10 9 8 7 6 5 4 3 2 1

Published in 2025
by
Christian Focus Publications Ltd.,
Geanies House, Fearn, Ross-shire
IV20 1TW, Great Britain.

www.christianfocus.com

Cover design by MOOSE77

Printed and bound by
Bell and Bain Glasgow

MIX
Paper | Supporting responsible forestry
FSC® C007785

CONTENTS

FOREWORD

The streets of Niddrie glance at me on my first visit to Niddrie Community Church. I offer a nod and a quick smile back. The brisk October air reminds me that I'm in Scotland as I arrive at what was once a mission, now a local church, on Hay Drive. A one story building welcomes me, white paint recently refreshed to cover any smoke stains leftover from the latest fire lit by neighborhood kids. I walk in, and I'm home.

Sitting at a table, Mez lights up with a familiar grin, cracks a joke, and offers to buy me a bacon roll from the counter. Within minutes, I am introduced to the others sitting in this little church cafe.

An older woman shares her story. Growing up in Niddrie, chasing a high was life. She remembers when Mez first showed up and how kind he was to her. He always made her laugh, but more importantly, he pointed her to Jesus. Now, years later, she's sober and an active member at the church. The man behind the counter has a similar story: addiction and hopelessness has turned into freedom and activity, employed by the church making bacon rolls. I'd hear more stories over the next few days as I interact with the saints at Niddrie, stories replete with hope and happiness. Not pre-planned advertisements or testimony reels on YouTube; these were simply regular conversation with ordinary members at local church inside a Scottish scheme.

Something is different here.

As we leave, an older man groans in fading inebriation slouching on the church steps. Words rich with kindness and continual invitation mark Mez's interaction with this man. Mez explains to me that the man had once made a profession of faith and even moved into Mez's own home, only to give himself, once again, to drugs and alcohol. He was ultimately excommunicated from the church for unrepentant sin.

Not all stories are triumphant.

Yet, even in this, I see compassion flow from this pastor toward a man in sin. Though removed from membership, he wasn't removed from their hearts. The man knows it. Stability in love compels him back toward these people. Perhaps he sees a love like none other. His story isn't over.

On a personal note, I first met Mez a few years prior and our encounter impacted my life. After one conversation with Mez, I left more encouraged than any conference on urban ministry had ever delivered. Ministering, myself, among addicts in Baltimore, Maryland and believing that the local church is where God shows off his glory, I found a like-minded brother in Mez. For the first time, I didn't feel crazy and alone in my ministry. I saw a pastor who believed the same thing I do about the church, but also one who dignified work among the world's forgotten, one who encouraged me to press on.

Back to Niddrie.

By the time I had finished my bacon roll, Andy shows up with his family. While Mez has a history with the streets, drugs, and violence, they call Andy "posh." To my American ears, I wasn't sure what that meant, but I figured it referred to a middle class background. What impressed me about Andy wasn't anything about being posh. It was how well he loved and connected with the saints in Niddrie and the sinners in the streets. His impact was untouched by his unexpected upbringing.

The book you have in your hands is written by two pastors who have done it. They have ministered faithfully among the suffering. They understand the power of addiction, but they also understand the power of the Gospel. Bridging gaps between the user and the never-used, the poor and the middle class, this book is practical and equips us to show true compassion and provide a pathway to sobriety.

We love our programs. We love our soup kitchens. We love our addiction ministries.

But what if we've become dull in the power of the Gospel? What if our love for programs has blinded us to the power of a healthy local church in reaching the addict?

What if the answer to the question, 'Do you have an addiction ministry?' Ought to be, 'Yes, we have a local church.'

There is a place for particular programs and soup kitchens. But Ephesians 3:10 doesn't say, "So that through *addiction ministry* the manifold wisdom of God is put on display." It says, "Through *the church* the manifold wisdom of God might now be made known to the rulers and authorities in the heavenly places" (emphasis mine).

Two pastors with two very different upbringings share one passion: they want to see Jesus magnified. This books offers a unique glimpse into the underpinnings of their ministry among addicts in Niddrie.

But this is not about Niddrie alone.

It's about addicts in Baltimore. It's about addicts in your own community.

Rooted in Biblical principles and shaped by a robust theological framework, this book is practical for every context. The book's uniqueness is not found in groundbreaking research or new programs, but in the centrality of the Gospel, the necessity of discipleship, and the importance of real relationships established in a local church. What I love is that you don't need a big budget or extra staff to effectively reach the addict. As Christians, we already have everything we need.

Reader, be encouraged.

Your community groans under the weight of addiction. Generations of users proclaim the magnitude of this problem. The pain is unbearable. Yet…

No longer must we drive past with windows rolled up, avoiding eye contact. We look directly into the face of an addict and see something very familiar. We see us. We see the root our own issues. We see the heart. This isn't Us Versus Them. It's not even Us Helping Them. Rather, this is a journey into the dark world of addiction so we might see the bright hope of Jesus Christ. Mez and Andy invite us to share their passion, that Jesus Christ be glorified.

I hope this book compels us back into our own communities with greater hope and expectation. May it help us better display the hope of Christ to the addict. As we learn from these two pastors, may words rich with kindness and continual invitation flow from our own lips to the men and women slouched on our steps.

And may our own churches be filled with stories of the Redeemed.

Joel Kurz
The Garden Church
Baltimore, Maryland

INTRODUCTION

My rude awakening – Andy

I had a sheltered upbringing. Born into a stable and loving Christian home, drugs and alcohol were not something that I really came across. There were a few people in secondary school who smoked marijuana and my brother struggled with party drugs in his teens, but that world was alien to me. I was a sensible young man who was scared witless of being addicted to any substance. I did get drunk once but spewed everywhere and never did it again. And I took one puff of a spliff at a party but decided it really wasn't for me. I had other things to focus on like school, football, friends and computer games. Drugs and alcohol didn't really appeal.

I became a Christian at the age of eighteen. After years of hearing the gospel at both home and church, the Holy Spirit opened my blind eyes to see that I was a great sinner and that I needed a great Saviour. A new minister had been appointed at my parents' church and he preached a convicting sermon from Isaiah 1 that cut me to the heart. On that Sunday evening, I realised that I was a proud, jealous, lustful, envious, disrespectful sinner and that my only hope of salvation was found in the Lord Jesus Christ. I vividly remember sitting on the end of my bed, feeling the guilt of my sin, confessing it with tears – and yet simultaneously feeling the weight of my burden lifted by the Lord. I was forgiven. I was free. I had become a new creation. And now all I wanted to do was tell others about the good news of Jesus Christ.

My excitement for the gospel was fuelled by the books that I read early on in my faith. John Piper's *Don't Waste Your Life* drummed into me that life was short and so I must spend my days wisely. And, as the old poem goes, I was aware that, 'Only one life, 'twill soon be past, Only what's done for Christ will last.'[1] I read also missionary biographies about people like Hudson Taylor, C. T. Studd and Jackie Pullinger. These books inspired me to take risks for the gospel and to serve the least, the last and the lost.

Cape Town

So, after graduating from Edinburgh University, I headed to Cape Town with a good friend, with a vision to reach gangs, drug addicts, prostitutes and prisoners on the Cape Flats and to see them changed and transformed by the gospel.[2] I had fallen in love with Cape Town and the Cape Flats while on several short-term missionary trips during the long university summer holidays. I had seen the need. I was inspired by the books I had read. I was young. I was unexperienced. I was naive. But I had a passion for the gospel and a yearning for the lost to be saved. What could go wrong?

---

1 C. T. Studd, *The Chocolate Soldier* (Deeper Christian Press, 2020), 33.

2 The Cape Flats is an area on the outskirts of Cape Town where Black people were segregated during apartheid.

Manenberg is a community that is blighted by gangs and drugs. Of course, that's not all that Manenberg is. There are many beautiful people who work hard and call Manenberg home. However, it is a brutal place to live. Different gangs patrol each corner of the community and it often spills into gun warfare. Prostitution is commonplace. Drugs are so pervasive that they are handed out like sweets. Poverty levels are high. The reaction whenever someone heard that I was working in Manenberg was always one of disbelief: 'You're not working in that community, are you?'

So, this white, naive, middle-class, privately-educated boy, with his other white, naive, middle-class, privately-educated friend, prayer-walked the streets with a local guy seeking to get alongside young men and share the gospel. Despite the reputation of the community, people were very friendly. We were able to get alongside four young men. We shared the gospel with them. We spent time with them. We took them away for a spiritual retreat. We even baptised them. Each day we met with them to disciple and build community.

However, the problem was that we had no idea what they were getting up to in the evening. One of the young men we befriended was addicted to a variety of street drugs and was a shooter for a notorious American gang. It shouldn't have come as a shock to me when he admitted one day that he had been using drugs (despite claiming not to) and that he hadn't taken a step back from his gang activity. But the news rocked me to the core. How could I have trusted him? Why did I not see this coming? How could I have been so naive? I had spent hours, days, weeks, months investing in this man, and it had all been lies. The experience woke me up to the reality that there is more going on beneath the surface in an addict's life than meets the eye. Addicts, like the rest of humanity, lie. It truly was a rude awakening. I had crash landed into a world I didn't know or understand.

Niddrie

After a year in Cape Town, I decided to return to Edinburgh. I was dating a beautiful girl whom I was ready to marry and I was offered an internship at Niddrie Community Church (NCC) – a church that was seeking to reach a deprived community on the outskirts of Edinburgh. After my year in Cape Town, I felt that I could do with some further training and the internship offered that. And I was excited that they were reaching the broken, the addicted and the poor in the community. So, in 2010 I started to serve as an intern at NCC.

I still remember the first few weeks serving in the church. Every day, the church has a drop-in café where people from the community come to get some cheap fried food and a cup of tea. Many – but by no means all – who came to the café lived in the community, were unemployed and struggled with a variety of addictions. The café had workers from the community – young ladies who worked in catering, some Travellers and a group of people who wore tracksuits, had pale skin and sweated profusely. To begin I couldn't work it out. Why were they sweating so much even though it was winter? Why were some of them half asleep and slurring their words? The penny didn't drop until Mez (who was senior pastor at the time) sat down with me and explained that they were heroin users. I had suspicions that they were using drugs but didn't know the side effects that came with heroin, methadone or Valium use. My knowledge extended to the addicted of the Cape Flats who mainly used crystal meth, marijuana and Mandrax.

Once again, I was entering a world that was very different to the one I'd been brought up in. I'd been to private school. I had two hard-working parents. I had been to university where people dressed in chinos and drank filter coffee. This new world – where many lived off the state, lounged around the café all day long and used drugs – was completely alien to me. I didn't know the difference between someone being high on life and high on drugs. I didn't know that while having a 'fag break' outside, users were dealing drugs with one another. I didn't know that the goods that were being sold in the café had been stolen from the local shops. I didn't know that when someone said, 'I don't take street drugs, it's just my medication,' that they were lying. I didn't know the difference between heroin, crack, weed, Valium, cocaine and methadone. I didn't know that there were four drug dealers within walking distance of the church. I hadn't grown up with the stuff and therefore I had no clue what was going on.

I was out of my depths.

A well-travelled road – Mez

My story is as far removed from Andy's as you could possibly imagine. My testimony is well documented in other books – and so, for the purposes of this book, I'll just give a short summary.[3]

I was born in Ireland in the 1970s and, for reasons still unknown to me, my father and mother split when I was very young. In our very early years, my sister and I were brought up by our grandmother and a large Catholic children's home. When I was about seven, we were shipped to England and

---

3 *Is There Anybody Out There?* 2nd edition (Christian Focus, 2015) and *The Creaking on The Stairs* (Christian Focus, 2019), both by Mez McConnell.

we moved onto an estate in Yorkshire to live with my dad and his new girlfriend.

My dad was pretty much absent during those early years. He was a builder who was out working all hours. When he wasn't working, he was in the betting shop or the pub. And then there were the trips to Germany with his building pals during the *Auf Wiedersehen, Pet* era of the early 1980s.[4] He was gone for long periods, and my sister and I were left in the '*care*' of our stepmother. She was a particularly cruel and wicked individual who made our lives a misery over a ten-year period.

Growing up, I didn't really see any drugs around. In our home (if I can call it that), there were just a lot of women sitting around drinking – morning, noon and night. There was maybe the odd spliff (or cannabis), but nothing like the industrial scale usage of today. I certainly didn't see heroin use until my mid-teens. I'd heard about the drug, of course, but heroin addicts were like mythical unicorns – people swore they'd seen one, but nobody could prove it!

Having said all this, I was about eleven years old when I first started experimenting with drugs. Somebody gave me a spliff to smoke and it was horrific. I absolutely hated it. I hated the sensation. It made me anxious. It made me paranoid. I could not understand why anybody would enjoy smoking it.

Unfortunately, this led to me trying other drugs, and by the late 80s 'acid house' hit our estate full force.[5] Everybody I knew, including adults, was getting high on LSD. By the time

4 *Auf Wiedersehen, Pet* was a hugely popular TV show in the UK in the 1980s about a group of unemployed builders from the UK, forced to travel to Germany to find work.

5 A hypnotic form of music which led to the widespread use of LSD.

we hit the 1990s, acid house gave way to the 'rave' scene. This movement was synonymous with ecstasy – a drug that, quite literally, gave its users an ecstatic high, and was intensified by the pulsating sounds of rave music.

This opened the door to all kinds of pills and drugs, which now became as easy to acquire as a pint of milk. Almost every single person I knew in this period was either dealing or taking all kinds of drugs, and often mixing them all together.

Life took a more sinister turn as we headed into the mid-1990s. LSD and ecstasy became cheaper and less pure. Dealers were beginning to mix the drugs with horse tranquillisers and even bleach. Several of my friends died of overdoses and many more began to experience serious mental health problems. Raves became increasingly violent as dealers fought one another for control.

Heroin also became much cheaper and was soon the drug of choice for those wanting to ease their 'come down' from LSD, ecstasy and amphetamines (speed). Heroin could be smoked or injected and most of my friends smoked it, because they didn't want to be considered a 'junkie'.[6] What they didn't know then was that heroin was super addictive, whichever way it was consumed.

At this point, the drug scene was my whole life. When I wasn't high, I was either buying drugs or selling them. It didn't take long before I turned to crime to feed my habit. Soon, the crime rate on our estate rocketed. Soon, it wasn't fun anymore. The raves had lost their appeal and now we took drugs just to stay mentally stable. My friends and I

6 A derogatory name for those who injected drugs into their veins. The feeling among my peer group in the 1980s and 1990s was that as long as you didn't inject, then you weren't really an addict.

convinced ourselves that we didn't have a problem as long as we weren't injecting.

One day I was having a conversation about legalising drugs with a local youth and community worker. I don't remember all the details, but I remember saying to him that drug-taking wasn't that big a deal: 'After all, everybody does it.' 'No, Mez,' he said to me. 'Everybody you know in *your* world is taking drugs. That's not the same thing as everybody taking them.' I laughed it off, but left with his words ringing in my ears.

As I pondered it, I realised that drugs may well have opened my mind – and even that was debatable – but it had definitely shrunk my world. I didn't associate anymore with anybody who didn't have or sell drugs. Without realising it, drugs had become my whole world.

Even when I ended up in prison at the age of twenty-one in the early 1990s, drugs were as readily available there as they were on the streets. Prison culture divided people into sex offenders, burglars, murderers, junkies and drug dealers. I naturally slotted in with the dealers. I was so accustomed to the culture at this point that there was nothing shocking if somebody sat in my cell and started injecting. It was as normal as drinking a cup of tea.

It was only when I came to faith in Christ in 1994 and began associating with Christians that I began to realise just how dark my culture was and how serious my drug habit had been. I started to see the world clearly for the first time in a long time. Drugs had been a cruel slave master to whom I had willingly dedicated at least ten years of my life.

What was normal to me wasn't normal. What I had regarded as harmless fun wasn't funny. What I had seen as something over which I had control had actually controlled me.

Ironically, when I came to faith in Christ, church culture was as alien to me as drug culture was to Andy. So, over the years, we have helped one another navigate these two worlds.

Why this book?

Addictions are on the rise in poorer communities in the UK. In Scotland, where we minister, addiction is a prevalent issue. Public Health Scotland reports that: 'Misuse of drugs is a significant issue in Scotland, and it leads to a variety of social and health problems.'[7] The most recent statistics on drug use in Scotland (from 2015/16) estimate that there are 57,300 individuals with problem drug use – that's approximately 1 in 60 people between 15 and 64.[8] In 2018, there were 1,187 drug-related deaths – 253 (27%) more than in 2017. These drug-related deaths, particularly among those aged 35–55 years, is now a substantial contributor to the worsening life expectancy trends in Scotland.[9] In particular, people who experience socio-economic disadvantage disproportionately experience problematic drug use. Council areas (housing schemes) with some of the most deprived communities in Scotland have higher rates of problematic drug use than the national estimate.[10]

Addiction is widespread and on the rise. It's important, therefore, for us to understand what addiction is and how

7 'Drug overview', *Public Health Scotland*, last updated 24 December 2021, http://www.healthscotland.scot/health-topics/drugs/drugs-overview.

8 Scottish Government, 'Section 5.3: Headline metrics' in National Mission on Drugs: annual monitoring report: 2022-2023, 19 December 2023, section 5.3, https://www.gov.scot/publications/national-mission-drugs-annual-monitoring-report-2022-2023.

9 Key facts, 'Drug overview'.

10 Drug use and health inequalities, 'Drug overview'.

we can care for the addicted person. The problem is that addictions are often misunderstood in Christian circles. Like me (Andy), many Christians have no clue about the addict's world. We've been brought up in places where drug and alcohol addictions are either hidden behind a veil of respectability or considered to be the problem of the poor, with whom we'd never engage. We stay in our safe middle-class neighbourhoods where our kids go to comfortable schools, where we have nice houses, and we drive past the rough areas to get to our respectable, middle-class churches. For many of us, the addicted person is someone to be avoided at all costs because they are just so different to us. As a result, many Christians neither reach the addicted nor know how to care for them.

That's why we have written this book. We have worked together in Niddrie for seventeen years. It's been a roller-coaster ride. There have been many highs and many lows. We've seen dozens of people from addicted backgrounds reached with the gospel: some have been truly saved and their lives have never been the same again; others have run back to their vomit and proven not to be one of Jesus' true disciples. This book is the fruit of our labour over decades of ministry among the addicted. We hope it will help readers think through what addiction is from a biblical standpoint and understand how to care with compassion and wisdom for those who struggle with addictions.

Some readers may already work with those who struggle with addictions – we hope you will be encouraged to keep going. Others want to start working in this area but don't know how to go about it – we hope this book will equip you to do so. Overall, we hope you will see that the addicted person is not someone to ignore or walk past, but someone to engage with. The gospel is the power of salvation for *everyone* who believes – whether they struggle with drugs or alcohol, or are addicted to comfort or envy. At the end of the day, we are all sick people in need of the great physician, the Lord Jesus Christ.

How to understand addiction and care for the addict

This book is split into two parts. Part 1 will think through what addiction is and what causes it. Society has tended to view addiction in terms of a choice or as a disease. Scientists and psychologists (and most liberal Christians) now tend to frame it in terms of emotional suffering and turmoil. However, we will argue that a biblical perspective must take into consideration the fact that humans have been created with bodies, minds and souls. As a consequence, addictions are best understood as an interplay between these spheres. Addictions are driven by sinful desires (soul), engrained by sinful habits (mind) and often perpetuated by pain and stress (body). From the outside, addictions seem to be insane – but, to the addict, they promise to bring order to a person's life. The complex nature of addiction is best understood as an interaction of sin and suffering.

In Part 2, we will think through how to care for the addicted person. In our church, we have seen a variety of people who have battled with substances find freedom in the gospel of the Lord Jesus Christ. The big struggle, however, is not evangelism but discipleship and caregiving. The addicted people who come into our building know instinctively that they need help. They readily acknowledge that they are sick and in need of a doctor – they'll listen and accept the good news of Jesus Christ with little persuasion. But giving up an addiction is often slow and painful. The addicted person has formed an attachment with their chosen substance – and that is not easily surrendered. They live in communities where street drugs are easily obtained. A war for their soul ensues. They need well-thought-out care, support and discipleship. As we think through how we care pastorally for a believer who has abused substances, we will consider whether there are particular things we need to counsel and specific methods of care we need to employ.

We have written the book together – drawing on the particular experiences and skills that the Lord has chosen to give each of us. Andy provides the theological framework for understanding addiction. We then apply it to various pastoral issues – Mez looks at 'Reaching the addict' and 'Training the addict' in chapters 4 and 6, and Andy addresses 'Keeping the addict' and 'Persevering with the addict' in chapters 5 and 7.

We hope it will encourage and equip you as you minister to those trapped in the slavery of addiction. We also hope that it will minister to every believer – whether you work specifically with addicts or not. At the end of the day, every believer is a struggler who must walk a path with others who are strugglers too. The Bible doesn't split people into addicts and non-addicts – it identifies us all as sinners, all of whom need the grace of the Lord Jesus Christ. As believers we all must learn how to serve and minister to fellow strugglers – whether that's the person battling with addictions or the person grieving the loss of a child. The problem that we need to correct is our view of the addict, so that we can minister to them as the Lord Jesus would have us to. We must see the addict as the Lord Jesus sees the addict – as a soul made in the image of God, broken by sin and in need of the word of life. We can all take part in this mission to care for the addict in our midst.

PART 1

THEOLOGY OF ADDICTION

1

WHAT IS ADDICTION?

Andy Constable

'This is the domain of addiction, where we constantly seek something outside ourselves to curb an insatiable yearning for relief or fulfilment.'

—Gabor Maté[11]

'For I do not understand my own actions. For I do not do what I want, but I do the very thing I hate.'

—Paul (Rom. 7:15)

If you walk through the streets of Niddrie in Edinburgh at around 8.45 am on a weekday morning, you'll see a string of parents returning home from dropping their kids off at school. There is a spring in their step because they are free from their parental responsibilities for the rest of the day. There is a buzz in the air.

---

11 Gabor Maté, *In the Realm of Hungry Ghosts: Close encounters with addiction* (Vermillion, 2018), 1.

Meanwhile there is another group of people who are beginning to make a move up the road. There is a weary but determined look on their faces. They walk quickly, but not in straight lines, often stumbling. They look unnaturally pale. Battered by life. Gormless in appearance. They wear tracksuits with holes caused by embers from their fags. Burnt fingertips from their lighters. Matted hair. They look like the walking dead.

Stevie was born and brought up in a poor neighbourhood in Edinburgh. Growing up, his dad was terribly abusive towards him, both verbally and physically. At a young age, in response to all that he was facing, he began to drink. Drinking gave him confidence and numbed the pain he experienced on a day-to-day basis. What started as an occasional drink at the weekend with his friends turned to heavy drinking every day. He soon mixed this with a variety of different street drugs: marijuana, diazepam, cocaine and heroin. Life slowly spiralled out of control as drink and drugs became the sole focus of his life. He could regularly be seen walking through his community intoxicated. He was banned from the pub and people avoided him on the streets. His family relationships were extremely fraught and he mounted up considerable debts with several different drug dealers.

Stevie tried a variety of different support groups including Alcoholics Anonymous and Narcotics Anonymous. He would muster up the willpower to stop for a few weeks or months, but something or someone would always pull him back into his addictive habits. After decades of struggling and battling, and with all hope nearly extinguished, he stumbled into the church one day rather gingerly, asking to speak to someone who could help him out. He was addicted, broken and hopeless.

Where are they going so early in the morning? They are heading to the chemist which opens at 9 am to grab their prescription – a heavy mix of Valium and methadone, which would knock most people out for six.

Who are these people? In Scotland they are known by the stereotypical term 'junkies'. They are heroin users. Addicts. Drug abusers. Men and women who are enslaved by a mixture of street and prescribed drugs. They are, of course, more than that. They are precious people made in the image of God. However, their addiction has enslaved them and robbed them of their humanity.

When we think of addiction, this is the kind of picture many people have in their heads. The dependent, enslaved person who has destroyed their life through their own bad choices. Often viewed as the lowest of the low in society. The broken. The hopeless. The wasters. The forgotten. The ignored.

Brokenness, hopelessness, emptiness, isolation – those are the effects of addiction. But what exactly is it? More importantly, how does the Bible frame addictions? I say 'frame' because the word 'addiction' is not found in the Bible, and yet it has become part of everyday vocabulary, even for Christians. It is, of course, important that we define addictions biblically because the way we describe or define addiction will determine how we care for the addicted person. And failure to define it biblically can lead to all sorts of unhelpful solutions.

We will look at a biblical view of addiction in chapters 2 and 3, but, first, let's consider some ways that society has traditionally thought about addiction. Three such systems of thought over the last century have considered the following theories: a) addiction as a choice, b) addiction as a disease, and c) addiction as a response to emotional turmoil. We will take them in turn.

Addiction as a choice

One of the most prevalent views of addiction is that it is a choice. This frames addiction according to willpower and the theory is that addiction is a choice which leads someone into an addictive cycle. According to this understanding, stopping is a simple choice. It is about willpower and self-control. It is the addict's lack of self-control that leads them to excessive consumption of alcohol or other mind-bending substances – and, since the problem resides solely in the person, it is just a matter of saying no in order to stop.

The strength of this view is that it recognises that forming of addictions involves the choices that an addict makes. Addictions don't simply form *ex nihilo*. It's not like an addict is walking along the road one day, suddenly trips over and finds a spliff in their mouth. No, there are choices that are made along the way which lead to the formation of an addiction. Bad habits are formed by little decisions that gather momentum.

This can bring hope to the addict because if they know where their addiction began then they can follow the yellow brick road to find a way out. And if an addict makes choices that lead to the formation of an addiction, then they can also choose to seek treatment. As Jesus says, you can choose the broad road that leads to destruction or the narrow road that leads to life. It's a choice that each person has to make. Further, it brings personal agency and responsibility in a world which screams 'I'm a victim.' Victims tend to blame everyone around them for their problems and end up stuck in the same pattern of sins, often angry, bitter and resentful.

However, the weakness of the choice model is that it can be too simplistic. The choice model comes from a view that sin is mainly outward rather than inward. It focuses on outward actions rather than a corruption of the heart. It doesn't address what we love and what we desire. It misses the vital category of idolatry. The Bible is clear that our choices flow out of what our hearts worship (Mark 7:21–23). The idols of our hearts lead to our outward actions. Choices flow from desires. So, mere choice doesn't explain these deeper issues of addiction.

Also, the choice model does not align with the experience of the addict. Addicts feel completely out of control. It feels like they are enslaved rather than making choices. It's almost like someone has taken over their bodies and they cannot escape. Therefore, mere willpower is not going to sort the problem out. Everyone knows this instinctively. Try saying no to a lovely piece of chocolate cake when it is in front of your face. It's not easy. Why? Because our willpower is weak and the temptation to eat it is sometimes irresistible. This is how the addict feels when presented with their chosen substance. But their temptation is even more powerful due to the way substances affect the brain and the reward pathways.

Finally, the choice model can lead to a Pharisaic spirit. Framing addictions as a choice breeds self-righteousness in the non-addict who sees themselves as better than the addicted person and it leads to isolation for the addict who is trapped in their sin. It is not biblical to see some people as having strong willpower and others as having weak willpower. Instead, the Bible says, 'The heart is deceitful above all things, and desperately sick; who can understand it?' (Jeremiah 17:9). *Every* heart is deceitful and desperately sick and *every* heart manifests that sickness in different ways. Some by choosing the folly of addictions, others by harbouring bitterness, or by gossiping and slandering, or by lying, or coveting their neighbour's stuff, or seeking their joy in money rather than God. It's not that some are sick and others are not, but that every human is sick and struggling and in need of the grace of God.

Addiction as a disease

The introduction of the term 'disease' as the main cause of addiction was essentially a backlash against the 'addication as a choice' view. Away went the idea of personal responsibility; in came the idea that addiction was something biologically wrong with you, a defect that you were born with.

The idea of addiction as a disease is very common, and the medical world in particular has homed in on this concept. The American Society of Addictive Medicine defines addiction as a 'treatable, chronic medical *disease* involving complex interactions among brain circuits, genetics, the environment, and an individual's life choices.'[12] Another medical journal puts it this way: 'addiction is a chronic neurobiological disease… characterized by behaviours that include one or more of the following: impaired control over drug use, compulsive use, continued use despite harm, and craving.'[13] For the most part, the medical world teaches that addiction is a brain disease or illness.

This language has been famously picked up by Alcoholics Anonymous (AA) and many other recovery groups. They teach that the addict's problems are not moral but medical,

12 'Definition of Addiction', *American Society of Addiction Medicine*, updated 15 September 2019, https://www.asam.org (emphasis added).

13 Maté, *In the Realm of Hungry Ghosts*, 128.

not 'badness' but sickness.[14] The mantra is repeated that, 'Alcoholism is a *disease* not a *disgrace*.'[15] AA writes: 'Through our history, alcoholism has been thought to be the result of poor moral fibre or lack of willpower... Only recently has research begun to reveal alcoholism in its true light: a deficiency disease, often genetic in origin.'[16]

In 2012, the comedian Russell Brand spoke to the UK Parliament and introduced himself as having the 'disease of addiction.'[17] Another podcast by a recovering addict states: 'We are born with addiction in our genetic makeup ... It's not my fault I struggled with addictions, but I have a responsibility to make it active. It's in our genetic makeup.'[18]

This is a very powerful argument because an addiction often feels like a disease that has taken over a person. Medically speaking, someone who is addicted to a substance has intense cravings and experiences withdrawal when they don't have their chosen substance. It feels like it is something that has happened to them rather than something they are responsible for. Their brains have become accustomed to the chosen substance or pattern of behaviour and so they feel unwell without it.

Usually, people who use 'disease' language have noble intentions. They want to garner sympathy and compassion for the addicted person. They want to move away from the

---

14 Linda A. Mercadante, *Victims and Sinners: Spiritual roots of addiction* (John Knox Press, 1996), 16.

15 Mercadante, *Victims and Sinners*, 17.

16 Mercadante, *Victims and Sinners*, 17.

17 Alan Travis, 'Russell Brand says drug addiction should be treated as a health matter', *The Guardian*, 24 April 2024, https://www.theguardian.com/politics/2012/apr/24/russell-brand-drug-addiction-mps.

18 Chris West-Russell, *Addiction and Recovery*, Podcast.

view that addictions are simply a lack of willpower and that addicts are the chief of sinners. They want to restore humanity to the addicted person.

However, there are several problems with the disease description of addiction.

First, disease language sees addiction as something done to a person, rather than a choice that a person makes. In other words, it removes the personal responsibility from the one who is struggling with addiction. The Bible however always holds us responsible for our actions (Gen. 3:12–13; Jer. 17:9; Rom. 1:18–19; Gal. 5:17; James 1:13–16). Addictions are not simply involuntary impulses caused by genetics or brain chemistry. There are choices, decisions and desires that lead to addictions.

When we reject the word 'sin' in favour of the term 'disease', we automatically remove responsibility from the addict. Eric L. Johnson writes helpfully:

> The 'sin' family denotes a disposition and set of ethical and spiritual motives, desires, thoughts, and actions that are abnormal for human beings: this is not the way it's supposed to be. Most importantly, embedded in the biblical words for abnormality are connotations of accountability, responsibility, culpability and relationship to the Creator.[19]

In a world where the word 'victim' seems to absolve a person of all responsibility from their actions, the Bible walks the tightrope between victimisation and responsibility. The doctrine of original sin has elements of determinism and human choice. It navigates a path between the voluntary and involuntary, responsibility and human vulnerability.

---

19 Eric L. Johnson, *Foundations for Soul Care: A Christian Psychology Proposal* (IVP Academic, 2014), 243.

Second, the disease description focuses on only one aspect of our humanity: our physiology. It restricts addiction to the realm of biology. The Bible however describes us as spiritual as well as physical beings. We have been created with minds, souls and bodies. It is too simplistic to describe addictions as a disease caused by our biology.

These differences can be seen when comparing cancer and addiction. Cancer is a disease caused when cells divide uncontrollably and spread into surrounding tissues. It is caused by a change of DNA. This is, in most cases, out of the control of the person who has it and it needs to be dealt with medically: chemotherapy, radiotherapy, immunotherapy, surgery and the like.

On the other hand, alcoholism or drug abuse always involves some sort of choice to start the addiction and to stop it. Self-control is needed. Neither treatments nor surgery can ultimately 'cure' addiction. It is a spiritual as well as a psychological issue. Biology plays its part – but, ultimately, the causes and cures of addictions can't be boiled down to a physiological problem.

Simply put, if the disease concept were true, then addictions would have a simple cure: medical intervention. If it were purely a deep, biological problem, then medicine should be able to provide at least some of the answers. However, prescribing drugs to help addicts has proven to be unhelpful. Millions of pounds are spent on prescribing methadone and Valium in the UK and yet it's caused more problems than solutions. In Scotland, it has been a giant waste of taxpayers' money.[20] Death rates caused by addictions are

20 Marc Ellison, 'Methadone programme "is a black hole", says drug misuse expert,' *BBC News*, 25 March 2015, https://www.bbc.com/news/uk-scotland-31943109.

through the roof, despite the medicalisation of addictions. Medicine can't solve the problems of the heart.

Even secular psychologists now teach that the disease concept is flawed. Dr Gabor Maté writes:

> [A]ddiction is neither a choice nor primarily a disease. It originates in a human being's desperate attempt to solve a problem: the problem of emotional pain, of overwhelming stress, a lost connection, a loss of control, of a deep discomfort with the self.[21]

In other words, there are spiritual and mental elements to addictions. And the Bible has plenty to say on both as we will see in the next chapter.

Addiction as a response to emotional turmoil

More recently, scientists and psychologists have started teaching that addictions are caused by emotional turmoil and pain. Dr Bessel van der Kolk has famously said:

> We need to talk about what drives people to take drugs. People who feel good about themselves don't do things that endanger their bodies… Traumatised people feel agitated, restless, tight in the chest. You hate the way you feel. You take drugs in order to stabilise your body.[22]

In other words, because a person doesn't feel well emotionally, they use substances to self-medicate for the pain they feel. It helps regulate distress and emotional pain. It covers emotional scars. It brings calm to their troubled world.

Gabor Maté is a Jewish psychologist from Canada. In his famous book, *In the Realm of Hungry Ghosts, he* says

---

21 Maté, *In the Realms of Hungry Ghosts*, xix.

22 Quoted in Matè, *In the Realm of Hungry Ghosts,* xviii.

we should replace the question 'Why the addiction?' with 'Why the pain?'[23] He argues that below the surface of every addict is psycho-spiritual despair and they use their chosen substance to overcome the anguish. In every instance, the addicted person is seeking to soothe pain or distract themselves from it.

There's much to agree with in this perspective on addictions. It is certainly true that we live in a world that is fallen, broken and fractured. We suffer and we feel intense pain. People use substances to medicate themselves against this pain. They use them to distract and distance themselves from the stress and despair of their souls. Many addicts have had abusive histories and experienced real trauma, and substances provide a way to cope. It's no coincidence that poorer communities are blighted by substance abuse. More pain = more reasons to medicate. As the UK Drug Policy Commission notes: 'Drug problems need to be seen and addressed within their wider social and economic context; entrenched drug problems appear to be significantly linked to inequality and social exclusion.'[24]

However, suffering is not the only cause. If pain was the sole cause of a person's addictions, it could be used to absolve individuals of personal responsibility and justify the decisions they make. While pain and trauma may contribute to the development of addictions, the intense pleasure and positive reinforcement associated with substance abuse also play a significant role. Addicts are not only sufferers but also pleasure seekers. They love their addiction because they enjoy it. No one makes a decision solely in response to pain – they decide what they think will make them happy.

23 Maté, *In the Realm of Hungry Ghosts*, xix.

24 Quoted in Matè, *In the Realm*, xix.

Explaining addiction as a straightforward response to pain overlooks the active choices and decision-making processes that lead someone down the path of addiction.

The emotional turmoil argument, by itself, is therefore an inadequate understanding of addiction because it ignores the desires of the human heart. We live in a world of pain and happiness, suffering and joy, sadness and desire. The addicted person is not simply self-medicating but is also seeking to find satisfaction in the midst of a spiritually thirsty world. As the Preacher puts it, 'I said in my heart, "Come now, I will test you with pleasure; enjoy yourself." But behold, this also was vanity' (Eccles. 2:1). Addicts are pleasure seekers who find that it's all a chasing after the wind.

So, what is the main cause of addiction? The root problem is that we are enslaved to sin. The human race is blighted by a spiritual disease that causes us to make foolish and irrational decisions. Every human is born in sin and so every human is fallen. The man who shoots heroin in his veins is no worse than the man who overworks in his job and ignores his wife and kids. Both are idolaters who are using their chosen god to justify the decisions they are making. The sin of the heart leads us to make sinful choices, it feels like a disease that has taken over us, and it leads to profound suffering – whether at the hands of others or done to ourselves. It affects mind, body and heart.

Therefore, none of these three models is quite adequate. None of them reflects the fact that we are body, mind and spirit, or the spiritual dimension of addiction. We will consider the biblical understanding of addiction in the next two chapters, first looking at what addiction is and then by looking at what the causes of addiction are.

Discussion Questions:

1. When you hear the word 'addict' what picture do you get in your mind? What people are engaged with these behaviours? What is wrong with them?
2. What are the strengths and weaknesses of the choice, disease, and emotional turmoil views of addiction?
3. How would you define addiction from a biblical point of view?

2

WHAT IS ADDICTION?

A Biblical View

Andy Constable

'Truly, truly, I say to you, everyone who practices sin is a slave to sin.'

—Jesus (John 8:34)

According to the Bible, we're all addicts. Yes, that's right. All of us.

That's how Paul talks about us in his letter to the church at Ephesus. We're not free. We're enslaved. We're addicted. In Ephesians 2:1, he says that before we were saved by Christ, we were dead in our trespasses and sins – in other words, we were spiritually dead. We were born that way. He goes on to say in verse 2 that we were following the ways of this world – influenced by our upbringing, peers, environment and the world in general. And we were following the prince of the power of the air. We were under Satan's bondage. According to the Bible, no one is born a completely free individual making completely free choices.

Who is the addict?

So that means the heroin addict is no different from any other person who struggles to say no to sin. As Francis Seeburger puts it, 'If nothing else, the spread of the disease view of addiction has greatly helped to overcome the illusion that addicts as a group are significantly different from other people when it comes to matters of ethics and morality.'[25] We are all addicts – some of us addicted to drugs, all of us addicted to sin.

Addicts are not aliens or a different class of people from 'non-addicts'. Yes, addicts lie, manipulate and steal – but don't we all? The only difference between a person who struggles with addiction and the person who doesn't is that the addict can't pretend to be what they are not. The veil of respectability and politeness is removed due to the desperate nature of their circumstances.

There are not two categories of people in the world – the sinful and sinless, the addict and the non-addict. The Bible is clear that 'none is righteous, no, not one' (Rom. 3:10). The Bible presents the *whole* human race as corrupted, sinful and broken. It is right to reject the concept that addiction is solely a choice and that stopping simply requires an act of willpower.

The word addiction today is understood as a dysfunctional dependence on a substance. This hasn't always been the meaning of the word. The Latin root of the word 'addiction' means 'to assign to'. It used to be seen in a positive sense: as in

25 Francis Seeburger, *Addiction and Responsibility: An inquiry into the addictive mind* (Crossroad, 1993), 68.

an activity that someone was passionate about or committed to. One could have an addiction to agricultural pursuit, for example. It was simply a habit or an interest.

However, if you go back to the Roman world, then you find the sense that we have today. An *addictus* was a person who defaulted on a debt and consequently became a slave. This gets to the heart of addiction: *slavery*. It is the act of attaching desires to something to the point of enslavement and eventual destruction. It's a dependency on a substance that is killing someone – but they keep on using it anyway. Jesus said that whoever sins is a slave to sin (John 8:34). This is true of all sin, but this is particularly pertinent when we look at addictions – they are enslaving habits of behaviour. The addict stays chained to a substance even though it is destroying them. As Jane Velez-Mitchell puts it, 'Addiction is the only disease that presents itself as the solution.'[26]

Gabor Maté puts it this way:

> Addiction is any repeated behaviour, substance-related or not, in which a person feels compelled to persist, regardless of its negative impact on his life and the lives of others... how does the addict know she has impaired control? Because she doesn't stop the behaviour despite its ill effects.[27]

Let's flesh this out a little more and frame it with biblical language:

> Addiction is a *sinful habit* that *enslaves* a person leading to their *destruction*.

---

26 Quoted in Mark E. Shaw, 'Is "Addiction" Rooted in a Disease, Demon, or Decision?' Biblical Counseling Coalition, 27 February 2012, https://www.biblicalcounselingcoalition.org/2012/02/27/is-addiction-rooted-in-a-disease-demon-or-decision/.

27 Maté, *In the Realm of Hungry Ghosts*, 128.

Let's walk through the four elements of that statement – sin, habit, slavery and destruction.

Addictions as sin

We need to be up front and centre about this. Addictions are foundationally *sinful* patterns of behaviour. Whenever drunkenness is mentioned in the Bible, the prototype of all addictions, it is cited as a sinful pattern of behaviour.

> Be not among drunkards or among gluttonous eaters of meat.
> (Prov. 23:20)

> Who has woe? Who has sorrow? Who has strife? Who has complaining? Who has wounds without cause? Who has redness of eyes? Those who tarry long over wine; those who go to try mixed wine. Do not look at wine when it is red, when it sparkles in the cup and goes down smoothly. In the end it bites like a serpent and stings like an adder.
> (Prov. 23:29–32)

> Now the works of the flesh are evident: sexual immorality, impurity, sensuality, idolatry, sorcery, enmity, strife, jealousy, fits of anger, rivalries, dissensions, divisions, envy, drunkenness, orgies, and things like these.
> (Gal. 5:19–21)

> And do not get drunk with wine, for that is debauchery, but be filled with the Spirit.
> (Eph. 5:18)

These verses are clear that any substance that leads to a person being out of their mind is seen as a sinful act. Those who get drunk in the Bible make foolish decisions. Drunkards are warned to not drink because of the consequences. And one of the sinful works of the flesh is drunkenness.

So how do we avoid the self-righteous spirit where addicts are seen as the 'chief of sinners' that we were looking at under the choice view of addiction? Well, we need to have a biblical understanding of the doctrine of sin. A moralistic doctrine of sin has been unhelpfully used to shame a certain group of people. However, the doctrine of sin is not simply about outward sinful acts but a deep spiritual malady that everyone suffers from.

When sin is talked about today, most people think of particularly bad or immoral actions, like murder. However, sin is described in the Bible primarily as an orientation that separates humanity from God, as a rejection of a loving and holy Creator. Sinful behaviours are the fruit of that orientation. Linda Mercadante in her book, *Victims and Sinners: Spiritual Roots of Addiction and Recovery*, helpfully writes, 'Sin is not primarily about right and wrong behaviour, that is, morality. Sin is first about orientation. One's *telos*, direction, primary attachment – rather than beliefs or behaviour – is what is most radically affected by sin.'[28]

It's not addiction that separates a person from God – it's sin. Addiction is primarily the fruit of a person rejecting their primary orientation or *telos*. The issue is not the doctrine of sin itself, but rather the misapplication of it. As Mercadante aptly summarises, 'For the doctrine of sin has been used sinfully, and we have inherited a very limiting version of it. Sin has been identified with proscribed acts, bad behaviour, immoderation, sexual license, failure to adhere to the norm.'[29]

The truth that the Bible presents is that *all* have fallen short of the glory of God and need His grace. It's not the

---

28 Mercadante, *Victims and Sinners*, 28.

29 Mercadante, *Victims and Sinners*, 21.

sin of addiction itself that ruins an addict's relationship with God. Their battle with sin is symptomatic of a deeper issue that the whole human race struggles with. It levels the playing field. *Every* person is a sinner. *Every* person needs God's grace.

Addiction is essentially a spiritual problem. It's not simply a problem of upbringing or environment, or the power of a substance. There is a deep spiritual malaise that we all struggle with: we are sinners in rebellion against a holy God.

Sin is deeper than the outward acts of sin like drunkenness. It is deeper than stealing, lying and adultery. Sin is rebelling against God and doing what is forbidden by Him. It stems from a heart that wants to rebel against God. It is a whole person orientation away from the holy and righteous God of the universe. And because our hearts are sinful, we commit sinful acts. Drunkenness, gluttony, drug abuse, sexual infidelity, gambling, pride, anger, envy and lust are all fruit of a rotten and twisted heart.

This is how Jesus talks about the heart and sin:

> What comes out of a person is what defiles him. For from within, out of the heart of man, come evil thoughts, sexual immorality, theft, murder, adultery, coveting, wickedness, deceit, sensuality, envy, slander, pride, foolishness. All these evil things come from within, and they defile a person. (Mark 7:20–23)

Sin flows from the heart and defiles us. It is not simply the behaviour, but the heart behind the behaviour.

And these sinful patterns of behaviour flow from what we worship. As humans we have been created to glorify God and enjoy Him forever. We either move towards that goal or away from it. The addicted person is someone whose desires are disordered – someone who is enjoying their chosen substance instead of enjoying a relationship with God.

Ed Welch helpfully writes:

> When you look at it closely, drunkenness is a lordship problem. Who is your master, God, or your desires? Do you desire God above all else, or do you desire something in creation more than you desire the Creator? At root, drunkards are worshipping another god – alcohol. Drunkenness violates the command 'You shall have no other gods before me.'[30]

The problem for the addict is not outside of them, but within them. Their actions are an overflow of 'false worship of the heart.'[31] The addict replaces worship of God with worship of a created thing and this dictates their motivations and actions. Idolatry is the means by which a person seeks to find purpose, pleasure or peace apart from God. When the people of Israel were at Mount Sinai and Moses was delayed up the mountain speaking to God, they erected a golden calf to worship (Exod. 32:1–6). What were they doing? They were seeking to find joy and happiness apart from God. They were looking to find satisfaction in something they could see and touch with their hands. This is what the addict seeks to do. They seek to find satisfaction in a god-substitute. Welch describes substance addiction as the 'modern golden calves erected by addicts to find meaning, power, or pleasure apart from God.'[32] Like the Israelites in the Old Testament, these

30 Edward T. Welch, *Addictions – A Banquet in the Grave: Finding hope in the power of the gospel* (P&R Publishing, 2001), 23.

31 Welch, *Addictions*, 49.

32 Welch, *Addictions*, 53.

golden calves enslave, control and blind the addicted person – and eventually destroy them.[33]

Addiction cannot be defined in the simplistic framework of a disease, a choice or a response to trauma. Understanding it in terms of sinful desires and worship helps us to see how the addict is enslaved to their sin – just like every human being. It drills deeper than outward actions, to the very core of who we are, what we love and what we worship. The problem of addiction is the problem of the human heart.

Addiction as a habit

Addiction is a repetitive pattern of sinful destructive behaviour. It's a habit. The Bible reveals that we are sinners who do sinful things. And these sinful things we do can develop into sinful patterns of behaviour or habits. As John says in his letter, 'Little children, let no one deceive you. Whoever *practices* righteousness is righteous, as he is righteous. Whoever makes a *practice* of sinning is of the devil, for the devil has been sinning from the beginning' (1 John 3:7–8, emphasis added).

Habits are extremely important for understanding addiction. Habits are the things we do that bring shape and order to our lives and they are powerful. In recent years, much has been written about the importance of habits. Charles Duhigg in his book *The Power of Habit* writes,

> Habits are powerful, but delicate. They can emerge outside our consciousness, or can be deliberately designed. They often occur without our permission, but can be reshaped by fiddling with their parts. They shape our lives far more than we realize

33 Welch, *Addictions*, 56–63.

> – they are so strong, in fact, that they cause our brains to cling to them at the exclusion of all else, including common sense.'[34]

Notice a few things here. First, habits shape our lives. They bring order to our lives and they become second nature to us. Second, they are strong. The saying that 'Bad habits die hard' is a true maxim. Once we are set in a pattern of behaviour it is very difficult to change those patterns. Third, habits are things that we cling to even if they go against common sense. Smokers smoke despite the warnings, over-eaters eat despite the health problems, and drinkers drink despite it robbing them of their humanity.

The power of habit is seen in Psalm 1. The Psalmist warns us to watch with whom we spend time. He says the blessed man 'walks not in the counsel of the wicked, nor stands in the way of sinners, nor sits in the seat of scoffers' (Ps. 1:1). Instead, 'his delight is in the law of the LORD, and on his law he meditates day and night' (Ps. 1:2). Right at the beginning of the Psalter, the Psalmist is warning us about the habits we keep. Will we spend time with the wicked imbibing their worldview or will we spend our time meditating on the Word of God? The Psalmist knows that these habits are important because they lead either to life or to death.

In his book, *Addiction and Virtue,* Kent Dunnington argues that the category of *habit* helps describe the addictive experience. As we have argued, he too rejects a simple 'disease' or 'choice' view of addiction. He maintains that 'habit' helps fill the space between the two views. Dunnington defines a habit as 'a relatively permanent acquired modification of a person that enables the person, when provoked by the

---

34 Charles Duhigg, *The Power of Habit: Why we do what we do in life and business* (Random House, 2014), 25.

relevant stimulus, to act consistently, successfully and with ease with respect to some objective.'[35] Put simply, habits are the everyday things we do that bring order to our lives. And these habits are formed in accordance with our deepest desires. In other words, they are repeated patterns of behaviour that are formed around the things that we think will bring us happiness.

How does habit fill the space between the choice and disease models? Well, habits are formed by choices that we make and yet, once entrenched, they become second nature to us. They are voluntary and involuntary, conscious and unconscious, intentional and unintentional. They come to us without even trying because they're formed around what we love.

For the addicted person, it's not a case of just drinking for drinking's sake – it goes deeper. It's an act of worship – a submission to something that promises to bring order, meaning and purpose to their life. We all have patterns of behaviour in our lives – things we repeat that bring structure and significance. Some of us have the habit of working during the week – getting up, going to work, trying to do our jobs diligently, earning money to pay the bills and heading home. This routine provides a sense of order to our lives.

The addict also has habits that bring purpose and structure to his or her life. In many cases, the drug, alcohol, sex or gambling helps fulfil that need for meaning. The routine of getting up to head to the chemist, on to a friend's house to share what drugs they have, going out to get money for the next day and planning how they are going to get the next fix brings a sense of order to their day. It's a destructive

35 Kent Dunnington, *Addiction and Virtue: Beyond the models of disease and choice* (IVP Academic), 62.

habit, but it gives a semblance of order and purpose. One of the reasons that substance addictions are so difficult to give up is because the person loses a sense of their very self and identity and purpose in life when they try to quit.

These habits are ultimately formed around what we love. As the title of James Smith's book puts it, *You Are What You Love*.[36] As human beings we have wants, desires and longings. And what we want, desire and long for – in other words, what we love – dictates our actions and behaviours. The addict loves their chosen addiction. They love the thrill of the chase. They love the hit from the drug. They love the pleasure of sex. They love the crisp taste of the beer. They fantasise about their chosen addiction and orientate their lives around it. Once they are in their chosen pattern of behaviour, it feels like they can't live any other way. It becomes second nature. They become what they worship. As Luther puts it, 'Whatever your heart clings to and confides in, that is really your god.'[37] In other words, we become what we worship because what we worship is what we love.

The category of habit helps us understand why addictions are so difficult to give up. If they are second-nature things we do, formed around what we love, then they become very difficult to change. Like sin they cannot be changed simply by trying harder. They will only be changed when the object of our affections is changed.

Kent Dunnington writes:

> Persons with addictions claim that their addictive behaviour is admittedly destructive yet, in some very real sense, beyond

---

36 James K. A. Smith, *You Are What You Love: the spiritual power of habit* (Brazos Press, 2016).

37 Smith, *You Are What You Love*, 23.

> the immediate control of their willpower. Similarly, the doctrine of sin teaches that human beings act in ways that are destructive of right relationship with God, yet those actions often flow out of habits and fundamental orientation that are not amenable to reform through immediate exertion of will.[38]

Addicts are entrapped by their addiction – and the addiction is further entrenched by the addicts' habits.

Addiction as slavery

Moving on to the next element of addictive behaviour, we consider the idea of addiction as *slavery*. The result of these deep, sinful patterns of behaviour is that the addict is enslaved – enslaved to their desires and to their chosen substance. Welch describes it as 'voluntary slavery.'[39] There are decisions that lead to the habitual patterns of behaviours that hold them in bondage.

This helps us navigate the choice–disease dichotomy. There are areas that we are responsible for (the choices we make) and there are parts that are pre-determined (our sinful natures). The result is slavery. It is bondage. The addicted person feels out of control. Unable to escape. Chained. Utterly helpless. It feels like a disease, but ultimately it's something they are responsible for. In other words, addictions flow from a sinful and diseased heart with wills that are in bondage to sin.

Think of a slave: a slave is not free. Their master dictates what they do and when they do it. The master is in charge and the slave must submit to him. The same is true of the addict. The addiction chains the addict and compels the individual to act against their better judgement. They know

38 Dunnington, *Addiction and Virtue*, 133.

39 Welch, *Addictions*, 32

that their addiction is killing them and yet they keep doing it. The addiction dictates what they do and when they do it. However, unlike a slave who is stolen from their home against their will, an addict is trapped by their very own decisions. They love their addiction and yet they hate it at the same time. Like a slave they lose dignity and they are unable to break free by themselves. Their cravings, withdrawal symptoms and inability to function normally without their addictive substance feels like a slavery. They are slaves who have sold themselves to their chosen master. And the sad thing about addiction is that the addict doesn't want to face up to the fact that there is a problem. They don't want to admit that they are enslaved to their addictions. So, they deny there is a problem and they lie to cover up their shame.

Alongside the slavery of addiction there is always denial and deception. The addict does not want to look at their chains and they pretend that they are not there. They tell themselves and everyone around them that they've got their addiction under control. They lie about what is going on because, ultimately, they enjoy what they do and they want to keep doing it. They think they are invisible and yet everyone around them can see that they are in trouble.

Even deeper than the slavery of their choices, it's important to communicate that addicts are spiritually enslaved to Satan. He is the cruel taskmaster who is the father of all addictions; he is a murderer who speaks lies (John 8:44) and addicts follow in his footsteps. He blinds them to the truth and wants to keep them in the darkness of their addictions. Slavery flows from the prince of the power of the air (Eph. 2:2) and he doesn't want to let his slaves go free!

The addict is enslaved.

Addiction as destruction

A final component of addictive behaviour is that this sinful habit, once it has enslaved a person, ultimately *destroys* them. Despite the effects on their relationship with God, on themselves and on those around them, the person keeps engaging in their sinful pattern of behaviour. Despite the fact that they are losing everything and everybody they love except their chosen pleasure, they continue in their addiction.

Maté defines addiction as 'any repeated behaviour, substance-related or not, in which a person feels compelled to persist, *regardless of its negative impact on his life and the lives of others*.'[40]

All sin destroys – but not all sin destroys equally. Addiction has a uniquely devastating effect. Solomon writes that drink and drugs bite like a serpent and sting like an adder (Prov. 23:32). He says the person who does not work destroys himself (Eccles. 4:5). The lies, deception and manipulation that come with addiction mean that nobody trusts the addicted person (Prov. 10:9). Addictions are like a slow death of the soul. In his letter, James puts it aptly: 'But each person is tempted when he is lured and enticed by his own desire. Then desire when it has conceived gives birth to sin, and sin when it is fully-grown brings forth death' (James 1:14–15). Addictions bring death to everything that is good.

Looking in the mirror

Before we finish this chapter, it's important to remind ourselves that the outward behaviours of the addict are a window into the souls of each one of us. The outward chaos, destruction, lies, discontentment, selfishness, impatience of the addict are a visual picture of all our sinful hearts. The only difference between the addict and the non-addict is that

40 Maté, *In the Realm of Hungry Ghosts*, 128, emphasis added.

the addict's sin is on full display. The veneer of respectability has been completely removed as their passions have taken over. The truth is that we all have sinful habits that enslave us and destroy us, because we are all idolaters who have loved created things over the Creator in different ways. And each one of us has the tendency to be addicted to any number of things in our lives. The seed of addiction is in every human heart.

Mark Shaw writes helpfully:

> The truth is that every human being on planet earth can become 'addicted' to any pleasurable activity because of the capacity for idolatry in the human heart. Do not underestimate the power of sin and the wickedness of the human heart.[41]

So next time you walk past that person who is quite clearly worse for wear – don't look at them and think, 'What an idiot.' Thank God that His grace has stopped you from taking that path and think about your own sin. Their outward actions give you a window into your own soul and the darkness that resides within. You are no better than a so-called 'junkie'.

Hope

Let me end with a word of hope: there is hope in the gospel! When we frame addictions according to the biblical language of sin and responsibility it means that we can point people to our only hope: Jesus Christ. He is the one who can break the chains of addictions and set people free. When people admit that they are sinners against a holy God, take responsibility for their actions, repent of the wrong things they have done and turn to Jesus Christ for forgiveness, then there is help. There is grace. There is unmatched power from

41 Mark E. Shaw, *The Heart of Addiction* (Focus Publishing, 2008), 79.

on high. For it is only the powerful work of the Spirit that can change our sinful and wicked hearts. He alone can make us new creations and redirect our worship to the one true God who created us and loves us.

Whether you are an addict who is struggling as you read this book, or you are working with someone who is struggling with an addiction, know there is hope in the power of the gospel. If He can change you and me, He can change anybody.

> Stevie stumbled into my office that Friday afternoon, intoxicated from drink. He told me that he wanted to change but didn't know how. He told me that AA had taught him to pray to a higher power, but nothing had helped. So, I simply told him that he didn't need a higher power but a personal relationship with Jesus Christ. I prayed for him, not knowing if I would see him again. But Stevie did return. He kept coming back to the church and different members shared the gospel with him. He eventually repented of his sin and put his faith in Jesus Christ. His chains were broken and he was set free. His life since then has been up and down. It's not been easy. There have been many bumps along the road. However, today he is not the man he used to be. He is married. He is working. He is making wise choices. And most importantly he is not enslaved to his addiction. Praise God!

Conclusion

This chapter has sought to answer the question: what is addiction? Since the turn of the twentieth century people have answered this question in several different ways. In past decades, some people saw addictions as simply a moral defect – something that people could choose to stop. As doctors began to examine the issue they diagnosed addiction as a biological problem that could be solved using medical interventions. However, over time, it became clear that addictions were more complicated than a simple choice or biological problem. Scientists and psychologists suggested that addiction was primarily a response to suffering and pain.

Although there are helpful aspects in all these approaches, the Bible tells us the underlying truth – that addiction is a spiritual malady that enslaves a person and destroys their very personhood. It is a response to a sinful and twisted heart where we replace our glorious God with the gifts He has given us. It is a habit that is formed in response to our deepest desires and loves. It is not simply a choice, because every human is enslaved to their passions and desires. It is not simply biological, because we are more than that. Instead, sinful desires become sinful habits that enslave a person and destroy them.

Discussion Questions:

1. The beginning of the chapter stated 'we are all addicts' – do you agree or disagree? Why or why not?
2. Why is it important that addictions are described as sinful patterns of behaviour?
3. How does the term habit help us understand why addictions are difficult to give up?
4. In what ways have you seen addictions – in your life or the lives of others – enslave and destroy?

3

THE CAUSES OF ADDICTION

A Biblical View

Andy Constable

'Insanity is doing the same thing over and over again and expecting a different outcome.'

—Old adage

'This world is not the Garden of Eden, and you cannot make it to be so. It is like that garden in this respect, that the serpent is in it, and the trail of the serpent is over everything here.'

Charles Haddon Spurgeon[42]

Addicts will talk about filling a void in their lives. They use drugs because of an insatiable hunger they feel in their souls.

Addicts will talk about how they are seeking to cover painful memories. It's a stress relief.

42 Charles Spurgeon, 'The Cause and Cure of a Wounded Spirit', *Metropolitan Tabernacle Pulpit* Volume 42, 16 April 1885.

Addicts will talk about the pleasure that their chosen substance brings them. *The joint felt good and got me out of my head. The cocaine gave a buzz and took me to a different world. The heroin was like a warm hug that I've never had before.*

Addicts will talk about the insanity of doing the same thing over and over and expecting a different outcome. They use their chosen substance to get a high even though they know that it's harming them and their loved ones. They use substances to solve the problems in their lives – and yet the addiction perpetuates a cycle of pain and heartache.

> Theo was brought up in gangland South Africa. He grew up in a family where his dad and his uncles were drug dealers. Drugs became the norm for him too. At the age of nine, he started to use marijuana, which one of his uncles introduced him to. Before school, he lit up his uncle's pipe with his uncle saying, 'Today you will be a bright boy. This will open your mind.' Marijuana led him to harder drugs. He ended up smoking everything from heroin to cocaine to crystal meth. He started manufacturing drugs. This was simply the normal pattern of his family. He smoked drugs with his dad. He smoked drugs with his uncles. It made him feel like a man. It made him feel like he was in control. It made him fearless. Once he was in, he couldn't stop.

When we listen carefully to the lived experience of the addicted person, there's so much more than a series of bad choices or a response to an awful set of circumstances. Notice in these descriptions that there is a godward element – my soul was hungry. There is a relational element – painful situations led me to seek something to heal the hurt. There is a biological element – the substance gave a buzz. Ultimately, we are more than our biology or our choices. God set eternity in our hearts (Eccles. 3:11). We are mind, body and soul.

We've put forward the view that, from a biblical perspective, addiction is a *sinful habit* that *enslaves* a person leading to their *destruction*. But we need to dig even deeper if we are going to develop a robust and useful way of helping those who are in the throes of addiction, experiencing the havoc that it brings and struggling to escape from its bondage.

We need to put addiction in the context of the whole story of God and His creation. Our world was once perfect. That's how God created it. He created men and women in His image, to enjoy His world (Gen. 1:27). He created us to live with key relationships – with Him, with one another and with creation. He created Adam and gave him a job to do; He gave him purpose and dignity (2:15). He created Eve – 'bone of my bones and flesh of my flesh', the perfect companion for Adam (2:23). Entirely equal, beautifully different. Together, they formed a new unit (2:24). It was mutually beneficial and enabling (2:25).

But then comes Genesis 3. Sin enters the world. It damages these key relationships. It damages God's good patterns of marriage, family and work.

And addictions are formed in response to the brokenness of these relationships and patterns. We will look at each in turn – our distorted relationship with God; our distorted relationships with each other; our distorted patterns of community; our distorted relationship with creation; and our distorted image.

Our distorted relationship with God – a worship problem

The central cause of addiction is that every person has a *worship* problem. This is the heart of everything.

God created us to be in relationship with Him. At the beginning, the Lord placed Adam and Eve in the Garden of Eden to know, love and worship Him. We see this in Genesis 3:8 when the Lord is walking in the garden in the evening with our first parents. This suggests that our forefathers had uninterrupted fellowship with their Creator. They talked with Him and they walked with Him and they were satisfied and happy. And this is what it was like in the beginning. Perfect fellowship with God. No sin. No pain. No addictions. Simply joy.

However, Eve ate that fruit and Adam watched idly by and sin entered the world, destroying this primary relationship. All the problems in the world, including addictions, are a result of our rebellion against God. The personal and relational problems we face are caused by a broken and fractured relationship with our Maker. The vertical breakage leads to horizontal wreckage. There's something in the view that addiction can be framed as a disease – but the disease is sin, not addiction. Sin is a genetic defect that humans are born with. It's a universal, pervasive, all-encompassing disease.

Sin leads us to wanting to rule our lives. We do not want to submit to God. We actively rebel against Him and His ways. In our unrighteousness and godlessness, we suppress the truth that there is a God (Rom. 1:18). We rebel against Him.

Sin also leads us to idolatry: we replace worship of the one true living God with the worship of idols (Rom. 1:21–22). Idolatry is worshipping anything we love, giving attention to something that replaces God. It's where we love the things of creation instead of the Creator. We move away from worshipping the one true God to worshipping work, family, comfort, control, sex, drink, drugs and a hundred other things. As Calvin famously reminds us 'the human heart is a perpetual idol factory.'[43]

Here's the thing: as humans we have been created with longings and desires. As Augustine said, there are three basic attributes of humanity: we exist, we know, we love.[44] This means that we love, yearn, want and hunger for things. Sometimes what we love is good – we desire to care for friends and family. However, at other times, we long for the sinful and it destroys us and those whom we love. We see that right at the beginning of the Bible story when Eve saw that the tree was delightful and took the fruit and rebelled against her Maker (Gen. 3:6). Or 1 John 2:15–17 which talks about the lust of the flesh and the lust of eyes leading to death. In other words, when we love the world and its desires instead of God, it leads to spiritual death. But the person who does the will of God abides forever.

And so, the question is not *whether* we love but *what* we love. As philosopher James Smith writes, 'To be human is to have a heart. You can't not love. So, the question isn't *whether* you will love something as ultimate; the question is *what* you will love as ultimate.'[45]

The habits we form flow from what we desire, long for and hunger after and they either bring life or they destroy it. The thing with addictions is that they are destructive lovers. They capture a person's heart and slowly destroy them. They

43 John Calvin, *Institutes* Book i.11.8.

44 Peter Brown, Augustine of Hippo (California Press, 2000), 377.

45 Smith, *You Are What You Love*, 10.

are like an affair which promises much but destroys all other relationships. They are like a boa constrictor suffocating the life out of a person. When our hearts are directed away from God, they lead to destruction and death. We are lovers who are constantly cheating on our faithful and loving husband. Where do affairs lead? Inevitably to the destruction of relationships.

Deep down, addictions are an act of worship. The addict is primarily a worshipper bowing to the false god of their chosen addiction. A god who promises much but delivers only enslavement. Author Bob Meehan writes: 'For the addict dope is God. It is the supreme being, the Higher Power, in the junkie's life. He is subjugated to its will. He follows its commandments. The drug is the definition of happiness and gives the meaning of love.'[46]

When people look back on their addictions, they often speak about an emptiness they were trying to fill. They use language like 'I was trying to fill a void' or 'I felt disconnected' or 'I was hopeless and restless'. This language points to the fact that we are designed to have a relationship with Almighty God and when that relationships is missing or broken, we experience the damaging effect.

Listen to the language of Jeremiah 2:11–13:

> Has a nation changed its gods, even though they are no gods? But my people have changed their glory for that which does not profit. Be appalled, O heavens, at this; be shocked, be utterly desolate, declares the LORD, for my people have committed two evils: they have forsaken me, the fountain of living waters, and hewed out cisterns for themselves, broken cisterns that can hold no water.

---

46 Bob Meehan, *Beyond the Yellow Brick Road: Our Children and Drugs* (Contemporary Books, 1984), 175.

The addict has forsaken their Creator and hewed out cisterns that cannot satisfy. As humans, we thirst and hunger for relationship. The only relationship that will truly satisfy that thirst is relationship with the God who created us. And as long as we are separated from Him, we will use anything or anyone to try and fill that existential emptiness. As Augustine famously put it, 'You stir man to take pleasure in praising you, because you have made us for yourself, and our heart is restless until it rests in you.'[47] Addicts are restless wanderers, cut off from the eternal hope of the triune God who created them. This is the essence of addiction. The addicted person seeks their soul satisfaction in a substance, rather than in their loving heavenly Father.

Our distorted relationships with each other – relational pain

Sin has also shattered our relationships with one another.

The Bible is full of relational pain. It starts within the first few chapters of Genesis. Adam and Eve immediately start blaming one another for what's gone wrong. Cain murders his brother. Lamech takes more than one wife and institutes a cycle of vengeance. Noah gets drunk and curses his youngest son for seeing him naked. Isaac loves one of his twin sons more than the other; Rebekah favours the other one. The younger son, Jacob, deceives his father. Then Jacob himself is deceived by Laban, his uncle. His youngest son, Joseph, is sold into slavery by his brothers, who lie to their father to cover up what they've done. Having been freed from slavery and on their way to the Promised Land, the people of Israel moan at Moses and Aaron in the desert. King

47 Augustine, *Confessions*, trans. Henry Chadwick (Oxford: Oxford University Press, 1998), 3.

Saul tries to kill David, his son's best friend. David sleeps with another man's wife and then tries to cover his tracks by murdering her husband. Solomon has a household of 1,000 wives and concubines. Imagine the jealousies and rivalries there must have been. King after king ignores the poor and oppressed. And that's just a taste from a few chapters of the Old Testament. The Bible is full of relational pain.

The two greatest commandments are to love God with heart, soul and mind and strength, and to love your neighbour as yourself (Mark 12:30–31). When sin entered into the world it turned neighbours into enemies. Strife, fighting, conflict, selfishness, loneliness, competition, abuse, envy, trauma, selfish ambition and pride entered the world.

Addictions are not simply caused by our relational breakdown with our Maker but also our broken relationships with one another. As we've noted, scientists are homing in on this aspect. Addiction is seen as a response to emotional pain. People are isolated, hurt, angry, abused, traumatised and so they turn to substances to *relieve* the pain and to feel *connected*. They feel bad and the drugs make them feel good.

When they tell the story of their journey into addiction, many will cite some sort of relational problem. They were bullied by their parents. They were abused by an authority figure. They were made to feel like they were not good enough. They didn't fit in. The addictions relieved the pain, gave them a sense of belonging and provided an escape from the realities and stresses of life.

> Stevie said that he used substances because he had 'low self-worth' and 'feared being rejected'. He explained that he continued to use substances because he was 'self-medicating his anxiety' and 'to forget about things from his childhood'.

He went on, 'As a child my dad was violent to my brother and mum. This meant that I was always hyper-vigilant. Drinking gave me confidence and numbed the pain I was feeling.'

Veryan said, 'I was depressed at a young age. Nobody liked me. I wasn't accepted. It was easier to be altered mentally than to be with the people I was around. It was self-medication.'

Tracey said she started her journey into addiction in response to the abuse she received from her boyfriend. She continued to use drugs as 'a coping mechanism. If life got stressful I used.'

Joe said that he continued to use drugs because it was the 'only thing that made [him] feel better. I would rather be stoned than face the reality that was going on in my life.' His mum was an alcoholic and was either never there or was violent towards him and his siblings.

Kim said, 'After I was kidnapped, I didn't know how to process things. I took to smoking hash all the time.'

Notice that these men and women articulate that their chosen substance medicated some sort of relational breakdown. They were fearful or abused or anxious or traumatised by the treatment of others. Addictions are often a running away from pain. Addicts are sufferers who are trying to make sense of the broken world around them, trying to navigate the painful relationships they're in, struggling with the painful world within.

When there's relational breakdown, addictive substances can take the role of friend and companion, allowing the user to enjoy being alone without the loneliness. As AA's Twelve Steps and Twelve Traditions puts it:

> Almost without exception, alcoholics are tortured by loneliness. Even before our drinking got bad and people began to cut us off, nearly all of us suffered the feeling we didn't quite belong. Either we were shy, and dared not draw near others, or we were apt to be noisy good fellows craving attention and companionship, but never getting at it – at least to our way of thinking. There was always that mysterious barrier we could neither surmount nor understand.[48]

When something happens to someone that is painful, their world becomes unsettled and uncertain. The chosen addiction distracts or medicates or numbs the pain inside. It's not always a pleasure-seeking exercise but a medicalisation of the mind and soul. Drink, drugs, sex, gambling, phone scrolling all seek to distract and distance a person from the reality of their lives.

Gabor Maté writes:

> All drugs – and all behaviours of addiction, substance-dependent or not, whether to gambling, sex, the internet or cocaine – either soothe pain directly or distract from it..[49]

Although Maté takes things too far in terms of social disconnection, he does touch on something that is helpful to understand – addicts are sufferers as well as sinners, seeking to relieve pain.

The Bible is clear about this. As humans we are not simply rebels but also those who are abused, hurt and sinned against. Psalm 10 speaks of the evil that often surrounds us, leading to relational pain: the arrogant hotly pursuing the poor (verse 2), murdering the innocent (verse 8), and

48 Dunnington, *Addiction and Virtue*, 118–119.

49 Maté, *In the Realm of Hungry Ghosts*, xix.

crushing the helpless (verse 10). In my community we see this all the time – fear, abuse, trauma and suffering leaving people crushed and at their wits' end with nowhere to turn but substance abuse. There is great evil that surrounds us, affects us deeply and leaves people at risk of addiction.

Broken relationships in the world are one of the causes of addictions. They don't often form in a vacuum. They are not simply a pursuit of pleasure.

Our distorted patterns of family and community

Leading on from this relational breakdown is the impact that sin has on our marriages, families and communities. The general environment in which people grow up is a significant factor in the formation of an addiction – and that too has been impacted by sin. God's intention was for loving, stable relationships to undergird the bringing up of children. Not that everyone would marry or necessarily have children, of course. But God's patterns established in the beginning were intended to lay the foundation for a pattern of honest, giving, loving relationships where people are kind and nurturing to those they care for.

With familial and relational breakdown, you'll often find poverty. With poverty you'll see a rise in addictions – not that addiction is exclusive to areas of deprivation, because addictions grip the poor and rich alike and there is pain across the social-economic divide. However, it is statistically reported that addictions affect poorer communities at a higher rate than richer. And the trauma often experienced in poorer communities can have devastating consequences. In 2018, the Adverse Childhood Experience found that children who went through multiple traumatic events were

7.4 times more likely to develop alcoholism and 10.3 times more likely to develop an injection drug addiction.[50]

Gabor Maté writes, 'emotional isolation, powerlessness, stress are the conditions that promote neurobiological addictions'.[51]

Substance use in family or community or friendship circles can leave people at greater risk of addiction. Kenneth Leech, writing in the 1990s, pinpoints the central cause of addiction, alongside original sin, as *social*. He states that it is 'too simplistic to see the spread of addiction purely in terms of personal responsibility… Instead the crack user's behaviour reflect(s) class, race and economic factors.'[52]

The Bible also talks about the impact our environment and friendship circle can have on us.

Solomon warns his son: 'Whoever walks with the wise becomes wise, but the companion of fools will suffer harm' (Prov. 13:20).

The Psalmist calls the blessed man to 'not walk in the counsel of the wicked, nor stand in the way of sinners, nor sit in the seat of scoffers.' Why? Because otherwise he will be influenced by them and imbibe their ways of life. That's why the progression is from walking to sitting. Before, he walked by those who were doing drugs – but now he is sitting with them lighting up a joint. Rather, he should 'delight… in the law of the LORD' and meditate on it 'day and night' (Ps. 1:1–2).

Paul wrote to the church in Corinth, 'Do not be deceived: "Evil company corrupts good habits." Awake to righteousness,

50 White, *Recovering*, 150.

51 Maté, *In the Realm of Hungry Ghosts*, 137.

52 Kenneth Leech, *Drugs and Pastoral Care* (Darton, Longman and Todd, 1998), 83.

and do not sin; for some do not have the knowledge of God. I speak this to your shame' (1 Cor. 15:33–34, NKJV).

The reason that the Bible warns us so forcefully about the company we keep is because we are relational beings who crave the approval of others, particularly our peers. We are social beings and others will always influence our decisions about right and wrong. Even though we would like to think of ourselves as individuals who are free from the judgement of others, most people care a lot about what other people think about them. Most of us have a strong desire to conform to the opinion of others. We can be like chameleons – we change depending on who is around us.

This explains why many people will talk about their descent into addictions in connection with their family or friendship circle. 'So and so offered me a joint.' 'I was involved with the party scene, and it was what everyone else was doing.' 'My sister was using and so I joined her.'

As Mark Shaw writes,

> The persons with whom you choose to spend the most time are going to be the biggest influences in your life. You will become like them because you will mimic their words and behaviours. Whether you realise it or not, you will be changed by their influence as you observe, model, practice and learn many of their ways.[53]

There was an experiment carried out on troops returning from the Vietnam War. The prevailing idea at the time was that the cause of heroin addiction lay in the power of the drug. However, Dr Lee Robins interviewed soldiers returning from the war and found that the access to heroin was more of a contributory factor than the power of the

53 Shaw, *The Heart of Addiction*, 89.

drug. He reported that while in Vietnam, half the enlisted men had tried narcotics and become 'addicted'. Nevertheless, when they returned from the field, only 5% of the soldiers who had used narcotics in Vietnam were still addicted once they were back in the US. It wasn't treatment that helped. It was simply the fact that circumstances had changed and opium was no longer available. The evidence showed that it was the availability of the drugs and the environment that the soldiers were in that had led to the addictions not the power of the drug per se.[54]

So, a combination of our family background and our general environments can be a contributing factor to the formation of addictions.

Our distorted relationship with creation

Another area that sin shattered was our relationship with creation. Adam and Eve were put in the garden and commanded, 'Be fruitful and multiply and fill the earth and subdue it' (Gen. 1:28). They were called to work the ground, to watch over it and take care of it (Gen. 2:15). In other words, they were called to care for the world they lived in and to 'have dominion' over it. However, sin reversed the order: instead of the human race having dominion over the world, the world often has dominion over the human race. Instead of using creation to glorify God, we use it to glorify ourselves.

This is seen again in the realm of addictions. The Bible calls us to be self-controlled and sober minded – but addicts use substances to lose their minds. Creation and created

54 Lee N. Robins, 'Vietnam veterans' rapid recovery from heroin addiction: a fluke or normal expectation?', *Addiction* vol. 88 (1993): 1041–1054.

things master the addict instead of the other way round. Our relationship with creation is broken.

Addictions are not simply a spiritual or even a psychological phenomenon. They affect biology as well. Everyone agrees that addiction changes the state of the brain. The substances that form addictions are used because they bring a pleasurable hit. Our appetites are strong. Think about when you have a cup of tea in your hand. What do you fancy having with it? A biscuit. And it's really hard to resist this. It's because our physical appetites take over. Or think about when you open your phone and you have 100 likes on your chosen social media platform. How do you feel? Elated? The most popular drugs are popular because they stimulate the brain. The key in substance addictions is the dopamine that is released in the brain when the substance is consumed.

Cocaine and other stimulant drugs work because they greatly increase the amount of dopamine available to cells in the brain.[55] In everyday brain functionality, the synaptic cleft ferries chemicals such as dopamine, serotonin or glutamate around the brain. However, when a drug such as cocaine is used, dopamine floods the brain and gives the addicted person the rush that they crave. This dopamine rush makes the brain fight the flood of chemicals by creating fewer receptors for transmission, which creates increased tolerance. Tolerance means the addicted person does not feel right without their chosen drug. This in turn perpetuates the vicious cycle of dependence and withdrawal.[56]

To get an idea of the buzz that drugs cause in the brain: food increases dopamine levels by 50%; sexual arousal,

55 Maté, *In the Realm of Hungry Ghosts*, 143.

56 Sonia E. Waters, *Addiction and Pastoral Care* (Eerdmans), 42–45.

nicotine and alcohol double dopamine levels; cocaine triples them; and crystal meth increases them twelve times.[57] In other words, these are strong chemicals that are flooding the brain. Plants were given for us to subdue and tend and use to the glory of God – but instead we use the plants to make mind-bending chemicals which make us high.

This again is why addictions are hard to give up. Once they become habits, the heart and body are enslaved together. The brain becomes hooked on the dopamine hits; meanwhile, the heart longs to be fulfilled. They go hand in hand. Mike Emlet puts it this way: 'Addictions are a worship disorder that often kidnap the body.'[58]

Our distorted image

We have thought about the impact of sin on our relationship with God, with each other, on our community and environment, and on creation. Here we examine how sin has distorted the divine image in which we were created. As humans we were created to be in His image and to be His 'vice-regents' in ruling over His world. There was a dignity to our humanity. Psalm 8 reminds us that we were made a little lower than the angels and crowned with glory and honour (verse 5). However, when sin entered the world, we were robbed of our dignity. We no longer imaged God. We became like a shattered mirror.

Instead of being orientated towards God and each other, Adam and Eve became orientated towards themselves. And one of the consequences of their sin against God was that

57 Maté, *In the Realm of Hungry Ghosts*, 145.

58 Mike Emlet, 'Overcoming Addiction', UK Biblical Counselling Conference, Seminar, 30 April 2016, https://www.biblicalcounselling.org.uk/video/overcoming-addiction.

guilt and shame entered the world. They were full of guilt for rebelling against their Maker and full of shame for their sin, and they tried to hide from God (Gen. 3:7).

Genesis 3:7 tells us that as soon as they ate the fruit they realised their nudity and covered up their nakedness because they were ashamed. As Henri Blocher writes:

> The narrative does not take up the word 'shame,' but the deliberate contrast between 3:7 and 2:25 suggests it immediately, and it is confirmed by the couple's behaviour. For what is shame, other than a feeling of embarrassment which makes us hide?[59]

Shame has plagued humanity since Adam and Eve ate that fruit and realised they were naked. It is one of the core consequences of our forefathers' sin against God. Before, they were in perfect relationship with God and with themselves – but, after eating the fruit, they were under God's righteous judgement, open to the accusations of Satan and embarrassed before one another.

Shame is that inner need to cover up when we do something we instinctively know to be wrong. When my children know they have done something wrong, they instantly try to hide somewhere so they don't have to face the embarrassment they feel inside for their actions. That is true of all humans. Shame is that inner need to cover up. Shame leads to hiding. Shame means we stay in the darkness. Broken communion with God and broken communion with one another turns into shame.

---

59 Henri Blocher, *In the Beginning: The opening chapters of Genesis* (IVP, 1984), 173.

Many addicts feel deep shame either because of the things they've done or the things that have been done to them. One former addict writes:

> There's a reason why doctors prescribe opiates after surgery: opiates numb pain. Similarly, heroin numbed my pain, caused by both sorrows and sin. I was abused as a kid and experienced the heartbreak of being sinned against. I wanted escape and relief. I also grew up in a church where I became aware of my own depravity. I wanted escape and relief from that too.[60]

Some addicts start using substances to cover the shame and guilt that they feel. And shame can keep people in their addictions because they fear bringing their habits into the light. Adam and Eve in the garden thought they could hide from God, as if they were invisible. And addicts also think that no one sees their chaotic lives. They become so used to the lies that they are deceived into thinking they are ok and they keep their addictions 'under wraps'. Shame means that people duck and dive and hide. That is why addictions generally breed in the dark where nobody sees.

Responsibility

As we end this chapter, it is important to note that whether a person began their descent into addiction in response to pain or due to their environment or an existential thirst that they couldn't put into words, each person is responsible for their actions. Yes, it is important to understand as many of the surrounding factors that contribute to the formation of an addiction in a person's life because it may be helpful

60 Justin Lakemacher, 'I Was Addicted to Heroin: Why Jesus was more satisfying', Desiring God, 16 February 2018, https://www.desiringgod.org/articles/i-was-addicted-to-heroin.

in their discipleship. However, the key to change is taking responsibility for our own hearts and our own decisions. We are certainly influenced by our environments, genetics and family background – but we are not determined by them.[61]

The more a person looks to their circumstances as an explanation – and justification – for the choices they've made, the more they can stay in a state of victimhood. This can mean that they never end up dealing with their own hearts and, therefore, they stay in a cycle of addiction. Those who take responsibility and don't blame their family, their pain or their genetics are much more likely to find freedom in Christ.

As Michael Horton puts it:

> There is no human being since the fall who is *only* a victim; yet it is also true that every sinner is *also* sinned against... It is true that we do not simply choose our vices, but are conditioned by the sinful structures to which our particular socio-cultural or familial contexts tend. Yet it is also true that we yield ourselves to these vices and are responsible for our own actions.[62]

After King David slept with Bathsheba, then lied and then murdered her husband, he didn't say in Psalm 51, 'It was the way that Saul treated me when I was younger that meant my brain didn't develop properly and so I did all these awful things.' No, he says to the Lord: 'Against you, you only, have I sinned' (verse 4). He takes responsibility and so finds forgiveness and joy and freedom.

The addict often stays trapped in their cycle of addiction because of the choices they've made in response to the

---

61 Welch, *Addictions*, 27.

62 Michael Horton, *The Christian Faith: A systematic theology for pilgrims on the way* (Zondervan, 2011), 427–428.

surroundings they've been dealt with. We must have compassion for the addict but that doesn't mean we absolve them of responsibility. Compassion means empathising and sympathising with the journey someone has been on, while holding them responsible for their actions.

One day Theo went to one of the drug houses in his community where he used to do drugs, a place where prison gang members and street gangs would meet and smoke drugs day and night. While he and his girlfriend were sitting there in that drug house smoking drugs throughout the night, during the early hours of that Wednesday morning, around 3 am, Theo felt a conviction that he could not go on with the life he used to live. He was high on drugs, committed an armed robbery that previous day, and having not slept for three days, he felt an overwhelming need to repent. He knew he could not continue with what he was doing; he felt so compelled it was as if someone was squeezing him into a corner. He turned to his prison gang friends and said in Afrikaans "Ouens ek is verdala!"- friends I am finished. They thought he was crazy. He said to his girlfriend (now wife) lets go downstairs, and as they went downstairs, Theo suddenly burst into tears. Turning to his girlfriend, he said, I can't go on with this life. Walking to the house on the next street where Theo had dealt drugs, he fell to his knees, called on the Lord, and was miraculously saved. As he stood up from his knees he felt like a heavy mountain had been lifted from his shoulders. From that moment, he never touched drugs again.

Conclusion

The causes of addiction are not simple because the effects of sin on a person aren't simple. As humans we are complex

– we're created to be in relationship with God, with one another, we're created to be in stable, loving families and communities, to be in right relationship with creation and to reflect the image of God Himself. However, sin has shattered all these relationships and patterns. Addictions are formed where this brokenness intersects.

As we noted at the beginning, it's important that we are not reductionistic in our assessment of the causes of addictions. With that in mind, let us conclude that addictions are formed where idol worshippers have encountered painful relationships they are trying to escape, access to the drugs and peers to share them with, and they discover the pleasure that the drug gives.

It's a combination of pleasure and pain. Of sin against God and being sinned against. Of pure ecstasy and misery. Idolatry and abuse. Sin and suffering.

Discussion Questions:

1. Before reading the chapter – what would you have said are the causes of addiction?
2. How does what we love lead to the decisions that we make? How does this help us understand addictions?
3. In what ways can relational pain and/or family upbringing lead to the formation of addiction?
4. What effects do addictions have on the brain and reward pathways?
5. The chapter stated – 'we are influenced by our circumstances but not determined by them' – why is this an important distinction?

PART 2

PASTORAL CARE OF ADDICTS

4

REACHING THE ADDICT

Mez McConnell

Tracey began her descent into addiction at the age of nineteen. Her stepsister was using heroin and offered her a hit in her flat one day. She had just been in an abusive relationship and so decided to take up the offer. She went straight from a couple of joints into injecting heroin. This decision entrapped her for the next ten years. Once she was in that addictive cycle, she didn't know how to get out again. It made her feel normal and covered the feelings of fear and guilt. When she was injecting, she felt happy, but this would soon dissipate, and she was left utterly hopeless. Life was chaotic. Her children were taken away from her. She was broken. She wanted to die.

How can we as Christians possibly help a person like Tracey? *Can* she be helped?

Modern psychology and counselling techniques offer very little hope to those struggling in long-term addiction. I know of many friends and some family who have been addicted for decades, despite the presence of a raft of care workers in their lives.

The power of God

In the Bible, we learn that the only way an addict can be transformed from the inside out is through the gospel of Jesus.

The world can talk about the power of positive thinking, or of self-esteem and belief, but it knows nothing of the power of God. 1 Chronicles 29:11–12 says:

> Yours, O Lord, is the greatness and the power and the glory and the victory and the majesty, for all that is in the heavens and in the earth is yours. Yours is the kingdom, O Lord, and you are exalted as head above all. Both riches and honor come from you, and you rule over all. In your hand are power and might, and in your hand it is to make great and to give strength to all.

Such is the incomprehensibility of His power that He formed this universe simply by speaking it into existence. But it's not just a power that is far off. It's not just a power seen in the immensity of a mountain range or the wonder of a clear night sky. It's a power that He makes available to those who know and love Him. We read in Isaiah 40:29–31 that:

> *He gives power to the faint,*
> *and to him who has no might he increases strength.*
> *Even youths shall faint and be weary,*
> *and young men shall fall exhausted;*
> *but they who wait for the Lord shall renew their strength;*
> *they shall mount up with wings like eagles;*
> *they shall run and not be weary;*
> *they shall walk and not faint.*

How, then, do we mere mortals access this power? How can we have our strength renewed? How can we know the joy of a soul that is at peace with its Creator?

This is where the gospel of Jesus comes in.

The power of the gospel

Paul tells us in Romans 1:16 that the gospel is the power of God. He says the same thing in 1 Corinthians 1:18. In Ephesians 3:16, he prays that the church would know the strengthening of the Holy Spirit *in their inner being*. Further on in verse 19, he prays that all Christians would 'know the love of Christ that surpasses knowledge, that you may be filled with all the fullness of God.'

Do we really believe that the gospel is powerful enough to vanquish addictions? Or does our gospel have limitations when it comes to this stuff? Is it powerful enough to save a soul, but not so good when it comes to dealing with crack cocaine? Is that when the gospel needs a helping hand from modern psychology or specialised addiction support groups?

If the problem of addiction is the problem of the human heart, then surely the only true cure is to be found in the only thing that can change us from the inside out. Do we, perhaps, need to re-evaluate everything we believe about gospel power and the presence of the Holy Spirit in the life of a sinner? Can the Holy Spirit do everything except keep drug addicts and alcoholics clean?

This is not how the apostle Paul sees it. In fact, in Romans 8:11 he encourages the church to remember that the same Holy Spirit that raised Jesus from death is at work in us. That does not sound liked defeatist language. If the power of the Holy Spirit can raise Jesus from the dead, then surely that same power can certainly free the captive addict from their sinful idolatry.

Just how powerful is the gospel?

Paul goes on to tells us in Galatians 5:1 that it is 'For freedom Christ has set us free'. Freedom from what? Freedom from our sin and freedom of the slavery to it. In other words, addicts are not a special group of sinners who are immune to the justifying and sanctifying work of the gospel.

The gospel is powerful enough to free us from the bonds of Satan. Paul reminds Christians what we were like before God saved us.

> And you were *dead* in the *trespasses* and *sins* in which you once walked, *following the course of this world, following the prince of the power of the air*, the spirit that is now at work in the sons of disobedience – among whom we all once lived *in the passions of our flesh*, carrying out *the desires of the body and the mind*, and were *by nature children of wrath*, like the rest of mankind (Eph. 2:1–3, emphasis added).

We were completely lost in sin. We were blind to our true sinful nature before our holy Creator. We were spiritually dead. We lived under God's holy wrath. There was not a thing we could do to save ourselves. We needed an intervention. And that's exactly what God gave us in the gospel. Paul says in verses 4–7 of the same chapter:

> But *God*, being rich in mercy, because of the great love with which he loved us, even when we were dead in our trespasses, *made us alive together with Christ* – by grace you have been saved – and *raised us up with him* and *seated us with him in the heavenly places in Christ Jesus*, so that in the coming ages he

> might show the immeasurable riches of his grace in kindness toward us in Christ Jesus.

We live in spiritual freedom and are saved from His wrath because of His power and His power alone.

If the power of God can defeat Satan, the world, the flesh, sin, and death itself, then He can handle opioid and alcohol problems!

Therefore, the challenge is to not lose confidence in it. *Do not be ashamed of the gospel*, Paul says in Romans 1, for there is no other power able to achieve such miracles. Do not forget that the gospel is not ours. We are talking about *God's* gospel. We are talking about the Creator of the universe and of every living thing within it. Creation works under the divine direction of His Holy Spirit. If we think of the world of addiction (and all sin) as a wall of impenetrable flame, then the power to extinguish those flames lies solely in the water of the gospel of Christ. We are merely the firefighters who direct the hose on to the flames through our gospel proclamation.

There is no greater power available anywhere in the world that can break the power of sin and Satan in our lives. Preach and teach it with confidence. Paul encourages Timothy in 2 Timothy 1:6–8, saying:

> For this reason I remind you to fan into flame the gift of God, which is in you through the laying on of my hands, for God gave us a spirit not of fear but of power and love and self-control. Therefore, do not be ashamed of the testimony about our Lord, nor of me his prisoner, but share in suffering for the gospel by the power of God.

The power of the gospel is so incredible that it has the power to change lives and even whole families for generations to come.

When I look back over my family history, it is a chronicle of historical addiction, abuse and early death. Children grew up under a pattern of violence, heavy drinking and, latterly, drugs. When I came to faith in Christ and married Miriam, all that changed. My own two girls (now married) were brought up in a stable, loving Christ-centred home. The same is true for our newly adopted son. The gospel did so much more than change my spiritual status before God. It transformed my family for generations. I sometimes feel that many Christians underestimate the multifaceted power of the gospel.

How powerful is the gospel in the face of sin and chronic addiction? It can do far more than we think and ask for (Eph. 3:20). In fact, we read in 2 Peter 1:3, 'His divine power has granted to us all things that pertain to life and godliness, through the knowledge of him who called us to his own glory and excellence.'

We may sit across the room from a wretched soul who has ruined his life, abused his family, stolen from everyone he knows, has lied and manipulated his way through life, and think: 'What hope does this person have?' In our theology we know that God can save, but in that moment it seems impossible. That's not how God sees the situation. He sees a wretched sinner deserving of wrath, for whom He has made a way back to Himself. That way can only come through His gospel. We are simply the medium through which He makes this offer to the lost soul in our care. Once preached, we must prayerfully leave the rest up to the power of the Holy Spirit.

Our job is not to save every addict that crosses our path. Our job is to trust in the power of God's gospel and to evangelise with all our heart at every and any opportunity.

The power of evangelism

We must make sure it is the *gospel* we are preaching. People are not cut off from God because they are addicts, or because they inject heroin. They are wicked rebels at heart. That is the nature of sin. The really bad news for them is that their addiction is not even the worst problem. God's wrath is. And they must deal with that at the cross. Once they are saved, and the Holy Spirit comes to reside within them, we can begin talking about how to defeat addiction in their life.

We must be clear that they are not victims of a terrible disease, but rather willing participants in wicked rebellion against their Creator. We are all sinners. Even the sweet old lady whose pension they stole is as guilty of wilful rebellion as they are.

When Paul wrote in Romans 1:16 that the gospel is the power of God, he wasn't trying to convince pagans of that fact. He was writing to remind *Christians* not to forget it. He wanted them, like himself, to not be ashamed of the gospel, regardless of how it was received in the world in which they lived.

Give them hell before we give them heaven. They need to know that God's wrath is revealed against ungodliness and unrighteousness (Rom. 1:18) if they are to ever grasp the goodness of the good news. Their need to be saved from hell is far more important than their need to be cured of their addictions. They need this power of God if they are to be saved. They need the Holy Spirit of God if they are to be changed. Without these things they have no hope of laying aside their idols.

How will the addict have the chance to change if they never hear the gospel? Paul tells us in Romans 10:17 that 'faith comes by hearing, and hearing through the word of Christ.' Someone needs to have the courage to tell them. They're not going to hear from a therapist, or a support group, or a methadone programme. The chance to change comes from hearing the gospel, repenting of sin and faith in Jesus.

If the sinner believes that, then they will be saved. If they reject it then they will die in their sin. They can either throw their lot in with Jesus and forsake their previous lifestyle and associates, or they can continue to lie to themselves by believing that their life is mysteriously going to get better one day.

The power of a local church

God gave us the gospel and He gave us the church – the worldwide Christian community of those for whom Jesus shed His blood. There is something special about local churches for local people. Local churches are the best way to evangelise and disciple local people. There is nothing ground-breaking or controversial about that statement.

Tim Lane says, 'A church community that understands that we are all fellow strugglers on the same path should be a very welcoming place for addicts.'[63] Being part of a local church reminds us that we are all sinners. Addicts are modern day lepers to many Western Christians – the kind of people to avoid by crossing the street. Yet, their desperate physical state is a mirror into the state of our own souls.

---

63 Tim Lane, 'The Church Can Minister to Addicts', *The Journal of Biblical Counselling* vol. 26, no. 2, May 2012

We need to fight hard to reverse the view that church is only for people who have got their act together. It is *not* a place for perfect people who are always happy. It is a place for sinners saved by grace. Behind every single smile is a story of wicked rebellion. As Lane points out: 'since the entire church is a community of "recovering addicts", and because we have a compelling message for addicts, it should follow that the church should be the best place for addicts to find hope and practical help.'[64]

The church is the place where they will hear the whole counsel of God and where they can fellowship with other pilgrims walking the same narrow path to glory. We must understand that there is a difference between running a support group in your building and being actively involved in the mess of one another's lives.

Being a church member helps us all to realise that sometimes we fall back into our old sinful pattern, that we need fellow believers around us. They're the ones who will call us back into relationship with Christ. So we need to submit ourselves to our fellow church members and sin strugglers.

The Christian, regardless of sinful addiction, needs the church as a fish needs its bowl. Neither the Christian nor the fish will survive long outside their home. The addict needs to know that the well-groomed family sat next to him in the Sunday service is as guilty of sin and secret shame as he is. And they need to know that they are as guilty of sin and secret shame as he is!

Christianity is a community affair. We are called to sing and teach and admonish one another in Colossians 3:16. In Hebrews 10:24–25, we are encouraged to maintain

64 Lane, 'The Church Can Minister to Addicts'.

fellowship with other believers if we want to grow in the faith and persevere in the face of trouble. Church is the one place where people ought to be honest with one another, instead of pretending that we have life sorted. If an addict is made to feel like he or she is the worst sinner in the building, then the church as a whole is not being open and honest about its struggles. The new convert needs the comfort of knowing that others sin just like them, but also of seeing and hearing of believers who have overcome their spiritual adversities and are persevering in Christ.

> Take care, brothers, lest there be in any of you an evil, unbelieving heart, leading you to fall away from the living God. But exhort one another every day, as long as it is called 'today,' that none of you may be hardened by the deceitfulness of sin. For we have come to share in Christ, if indeed we hold our original confidence firm to the end. (Heb. 3:12–14)

Coming together in worship regularly with other sinners stops us from the sin of identifying ourselves by our prevailing struggle. I'm an addict, a homosexual, a gambler or a gossip. These sins are what we *do*, but fellowship in the church teaches that this is not who we *are*. In Christ, we are new creations (2 Cor. 5:17). Betty may not know what it is like to chase the dragon or know what cold turkey feels like, but she knows the struggle of the flesh within. Her addiction to online Bingo may be well hidden by a friendly smile, some nice perfume and nice clothing. But she is a sinner, nonetheless. No better than you or I.

Here's the thing: the local church offers the best platform for people to hear the gospel. Every community needs a localised lampstand, shining forth the gospel of Jesus. Sinners need to hear the message of repentance and faith, but they also need to see it lived out in their own contexts. If people only get to hear the gospel a couple of times a week, but don't have a visible means of seeing how the faith should be lived out in the everyday, how is that going to be helpful in building a strong, robust faith?

But evangelism also flows out of relationship. It flows from a loving community. How can people see the love of Christ if Christians only gather in a building for a few meetings each week?

Most of our evangelistic conversations happen in everyday life. Most of the people we've seen converted come from everyday ministries on the ground. They have come through a recovery Bible study group or the café or our football team or a friend inviting them to church or youth work. It's taken time and effort to win souls for Christ.

The Lord Jesus loves the church. A God-glorifying, Bible-believing, gospel-preaching, actively discipling, healthy, local church living in Christian community, serving and loving one another is going to make an impact in any community. It is what the world desperately needs. Even a small, tight-knit band of brothers and sisters is going to bring about cultural and community renewal. What a home it will be for – not just addicts – but all the weary and broken who will come to Christ for salvation.

Tracey was addicted. Her life was all over the place and it looked like she had no way out. Her children were taken from her and she was at an all-time low, questioning whether she even wanted to keep on living. However, one day she heard that a new minister had taken over at Niddrie Community Church. He had struggled with drugs and had found freedom and she thought maybe the same could be true for her. A lady from church called Sharon met Tracey and started to study the Bible with her. She shared the hope of the gospel with her and Tracey submitted her life to the Lord Jesus Christ. She immediately felt relieved. She knew that the price had been paid for her sin and this brought great relief. Her chains were gone and she didn't need to feel guilty anymore. Soon after, she went to a family-run Christian rehabilitation house. This allowed her to grow as a Christian away from the temptations of Niddrie and the drug scene there. She was supported by a variety of different families from the church and she grew and changed. Now she is a member of Niddrie, she is married to a lovely Christian man, one of her sons is saved, and she works full time caring for others. All praise to King Jesus!

Conclusion

The power of a local church, preaching the powerful gospel of the powerful Creator of this world is an irresistible force to those whom He calls to salvation. Those whom we once crossed the street to avoid become beloved brothers and sisters in Jesus. Not only do we learn to love one another, we learn to live with and encourage one another in the fight of faith.

The polished middle-class housewife realises that her soul is no different from the ragged, pasty-faced crack addict. The businessman realises that his self-righteousness is as ugly to God as the stumbling alcoholic's addiction. The pastor learns that he can learn humility and honest confession from the biblically illiterate gambling addict. All of our lives can be enriched as we sit under the power of the gospel and encourage each other to Christlikeness on our journey to the Promised Land, where one day the thief will worship with the judge, the junkie with the pharmacist, the gambler with the accountant, the bin man with the lawyer, the lion with the lamb.

And it will be glorious.

Discussion Questions:

1. Paul writes, 'For I am not ashamed of the gospel, for it is the power of God for salvation to everyone who believes…' (Rom. 1:16). Why do you think people are tempted to lose confidence in the gospel when it comes to addictions?
2. Why is the local church vital for believers to grow as disciples of Jesus Christ? In what ways can recovery groups and rehabs strengthen the church? Are there ways that recovery groups and rehabs can weaken the church?

5

KEEPING THE ADDICT

Andy Constable

They devoted themselves to the apostles' teaching, to the fellowship, to the breaking of bread, and to prayer... Every day they devoted themselves to meeting together in the temple, and broke bread from house to house.

—Acts 2:42, 46a CSB

Creating "home" takes a huge personal and relational investment that engages people physically, socially, emotionally, psychologically, practically, politically, and spiritually.

—Aaron White[65]

Kim was brought up in the Traveller community in Edinburgh. The first time she did drugs she was twelve and she smoked hash with pals while drinking. It wasn't heavy to begin with – it was just a social thing that she did. She casually

65 White, *Recovering*, 46.

took ecstasy and then speed, which her sister gave her. This all turned when her dad kidnapped her. She didn't know how to process things and so took to smoking hash all the time. She then began to drink heavily at the weekends. Amphetamines. Chaos ensued. The party drugs of ecstasy and speed stopped working for her. She then turned to downers – heroin and crack – to numb things. These drugs numbed her feelings and covered her disappointments and the heaviness of life. The drugs made her life more bearable while robbing her of her respectability at the same time. Life was full of issues, pain and heartache. Life wasn't working for her, so she called out to the Lord. That next weekend, half cut, she turned up at Niddrie Community Church looking for help.

She heard the gospel that Sunday and committed her life to follow Christ. The heaviness of her sins were immediately relieved. She started to turn up to church each day. Someone would meet with her to study the Bible and help her understand what it meant to follow Christ. She was also given a schedule to structure her week which included working in the café, team meetings and cleaning the church. This kept her hands busy and around people who would keep her accountable. There were many battles in those early years. The world tried to pull her back and her flesh gave into her desires. But slowly and surely, with the help of a healthy local church which provided the Word of God, intensive discipleship, structure and accountability, she grew spiritually and said goodbye to her substance addictions.

When I became a Christian, I wasn't a big fan of the church. Like many of my generation I hated authority. I hated the idea of formalised religion. I thought that structure and formalism killed the Spirit. I thought all I needed to do was to share the gospel, love people and the rest would take care of itself. Who needs the church? Who needs structure? Who needs membership? Who needs church discipline? Can't we just love Jesus and be done with all this church stuff?

Then I went to South Africa to do ministry with a para-church organisation. We did prayer ministry on the streets. We would preach the gospel to drug addicts and gang members. And we saw people get converted. People responded to the gospel. We baptised four. We discipled them as best as we could. But as we went on, here was the problem: these young men needed discipleship. They needed structure.

We were faced with some difficult issues. What do you do with someone when they fall into serious sin after being baptised? What happens when the person who professes faith is sleeping around? What do you do when the person who professes faith is part of a gang and still smokes drugs at night? What authority did we have to challenge them? And how do you tell the community that that person is no longer living up to their profession of faith? How do you protect the purity of the gospel? These questions troubled me.

On top of that, I couldn't give these men what they needed, nor could the few others who were also struggling with addictions. They needed a group of believers from different backgrounds, with different experiences, from different generations who were covenanted together to teach them the Bible, love them well and keep them accountable so that they were able to flourish and grow. These men needed the church. A healthy gospel-preaching church.

This is what every believer needs whether they have struggled with drink and drugs in their past or not. It is the means that God uses to grow healthy, God-fearing Christians.

So how can the church keep the addict? The church is the place to disciple the addict, but are there particular means we need to use in order to disciple effectively? Yes and no. The addict is like every other idolater and so the means of grace (word, prayer, community, etc.) to keep the addict is the same as any other believer. However, like any besetting sin, there are particular applications of God's grace that we need to think through when discipling the addict.

The power of consistent and consecutive Bible teaching

Jesus' main ministry to his disciples was to teach them about Himself. He taught them the Word. He taught them about the kingdom of God and what it looked like. He taught them about who He was and why He had come. He taught them about the end and what it was going to look like. He didn't hold back on anything. He said to his disciples after a spate of miracles, 'Let us go on to the next towns, that I may preach there also, for that is why I came out' (Mark 1:38).

And then when Jesus sent his guys out, He told them to do the same: Go and *make disciples*, baptizing them and teaching them all that I have commanded (Matt. 28:19-20, emphasis added). So, think about what He did. He spent three years with His disciples teaching them all about Himself and then He sent them out to do the same.

And this is what we see throughout the New Testament. The first disciples went out into the world and preached the gospel and then discipled people through teaching them Jesus' words. When Paul spent time with new Christians in Ephesus, he said this at the end of their time together: 'Therefore I testify to you this day that I am innocent of the blood of all, for I did not shrink from declaring to you the whole counsel of God' (Acts 20:26–27). Paul was innocent of their blood because he had taught them the whole will of God – that's everything they needed to know about the Bible. He didn't share the gospel and then leave them there. He taught them until they understood all of God's Word.

He said this about his work among the Colossian Christians: 'Him we proclaim, warning and teaching everyone with all wisdom, that we may present everyone mature in Christ. For this I toil, struggling with all his energy that he powerfully works in me' (Col. 1:28-29). Paul struggled with all his energy to present Christians mature in Christ! As before, he didn't just preach the gospel and then say to them, 'Good to spend time with you, brothers and sisters, I'm off – but I'll pray for you!' No, he agonised over them, he kicked them up the backside when they were chasing after false doctrine, he encouraged them when they needed comfort, and he reminded them of the truth of Jesus' teachings again and again and again and again. He wanted with all his might to see his brothers and sisters mature in Christ.

So, if we want to see men and women put their addictions to death then they will need to understand God's Word. They need to delight in God's Word because this is what will sustain them as they live in the freedom that Christ has purchased them. Psalm 1:1–2 says, 'Blessed is the man… [whose] delight is in the law of the LORD, and on his law he meditates day and night.' The Psalmist asks, 'How can a young man keep his way pure?' And the answer is: 'By guarding it according to your word… I have stored up your word in my heart, that I might not sin against you' (Ps. 119:9, 11).

The lie that recovery groups have espoused is that addicts need a special form of discipleship. They need AA's *Big Book* and special recovery meetings for them to stay away from their addictions. However, the Bible does not give us a special discipleship path for addicts and something different for everyone else. No, all of us need the Word of God. Plain and simple.

It is the Word that brings life. It is the Word that convicts sinners. It is the Word that is the spiritual food Christians need to grow.

The addict therefore needs to listen to and meditate on God's Word so that they can grow spiritually and have the tools they need to fight their addictions. This is important because they need to rely on God, not on those who are caring for them. Sometimes those struggling with addictions get so fixated on their recovery meetings or having that person in their life to care for them that they become dependent on them. However, this can become an unhealthy habit. The addict needs to depend on God, not on their recovery workers or pastoral carers. They need to grow and learn to walk by themselves. Otherwise, our helping can become hurting.[66] It can lead to an unhealthy dependence on other people instead of God.

In Niddrie, we have found that people are hungry for God's Word. Our new Christians will sit down and listen to a sermon for thirty or forty minutes. They will take part in a Bible study for an hour. No thrills – just wanting to listen to God's Word clearly explained.

If we withhold God's Word from people, we spiritually starve them. As Jesus quoted to the devil, 'Man shall not live by bread alone, but by every word that comes from the mouth of God' (Matt. 4:4).

Addicts long for God – just like the Psalmist.[67] They too are deeply spiritually thirsty. Those that have been set

66 More on this later.

67 Psalm 42.

free from the chains of addictions need to feast on Christ through His eternal Word. Pastoral carers need to hold out God's eternal truth like Jesus did. He didn't water down truth. He gave His disciples difficult things to think about. He fried their brains. He didn't hold back. In the same way, we need to teach our disciples from difficult backgrounds the whole counsel of God.

Sometimes we don't know where to start. Do we challenge the addiction, the sexual immorality, the stealing from the local shop, the misuse of money, the gossiping? It's hard to know.

When we teach the whole counsel of God, it will prod and convict those we are discipling as the Spirit works in their lives on all sorts of levels. Addicts don't struggle with just one issue, but all sorts of sin issues – like everyone else. One person said to me, 'I thought I just had an addiction problem but now I've come to Christ, I've realised I've got layer upon layer of sin.' We need to get to the heart of people, and we do this through the consistent teaching of the Word of God.

I remember when we had several people come to Christ a few years ago. It was mad. These new converts were fighting. They were taking drugs. They were gossiping. They were sleeping with one another. They were all at it. And I kept thinking, how are we going to sort this out? And the answer was just continuing to teach God's Word, keep challenging sin and let God do His thing. We did a series on 1 Corinthians and God challenged a lot of hearts. Those who were Christians moved on with the Lord while those who were just playing around stopped coming. God worked through the teaching of His Word.

The power of a loving community

The early church met every day to break bread, hear God's Word and have fellowship with one another. This is the kind of fellowship the new Christian needs, whatever their background, but especially the person who is putting to death their addictions.

Addicts tend to spend time with other addicts. There is a camaraderie that binds the community of addicts together. They are on the same mission (the use of the substance) with a code of conduct (dos and don'ts) and an acceptance of what each other is doing. In a way, they act like a family, albeit a very dysfunctional one. Yes, they manipulate, steal and lie to one another, but who else have they got? Their biological families have turned their backs on them and society has shunned them.

So, when the addicted person is seeking to give up their addiction, they are also giving up their family. They are losing their friendship circle. In a sense, they are giving up all they know. A piece of their identity is put to death. Their friends will try to tempt them back and, in their weak moments, they might return to their vomit. That is why the addict needs a new family. They need a loving church family to come around them and show them what true community looks like. To offer friendship and support. To teach them God's ways. To show them God's ways. To train them in God's ways.

The early church was not perfect. They were beset with problems. However, they loved one another well. They didn't simply meet on a Sunday for an hour and that was it. No, they met daily. They shared life with one another. They shared all that they had (Acts 2:42–47). This is what true Christian community looks like. The problem in the West is that an individualistic mindset has infected the church. Instead of sharing life together, Christians have put up drawbridges. Instead of meeting regularly, Christians find any reason not to meet. Instead of honest, vulnerable relationships Christians (particularly from affluent backgrounds) are reserved, often protecting a veneer of respectability. That is not family or gospel community. And it's certainly not going to help the guy struggling with alcoholism or the lady battling with a heroin addiction.

The addicted person needs an honest community where people are open about their weaknesses and struggles.

The addicted person needs daily fellowship, especially in the early years, so that they can feast on God's Word and know the love of fellow disciples.

The addicted person needs to be kept busy so that their idleness does not make light work for the devil.

The addicted person needs to be picked up like a toddler when they stumble and fall.

The addicted person needs to be loved through the ups and downs of life. When they are struggling or when they are being selfish or when they are just feeling alone and tempted to play with fire, they need those loving brothers and sisters of their fellowship to notice them and come alongside them.

This is what we saw in Kim's testimony at the beginning: she needed the church to stick with her and help her grow. She needed people to show her how to be a godly parent. She needed people to help her make wise decisions. She needed people to keep her accountable and challenge her when she was in sin. She needed structure to her week. But most importantly she needed a Christian family! She needed the whole body of Christ to love her and her children.

Therefore, Kim, and every addict, need more than a weekly meeting. They need daily discipleship.

Kent Dunnington commenting on the need for church community for the addict writes:

> The importance of place and 'dailyness' for the success of AA cannot be overstated… If the church is to be a place where addicted persons may find redeeming fellowship, it will have to become a primary social hub.[68]

Dunnington emphasises the importance of a social community that functions every day:

> But if the church is to provide a genuine alternative to addicted persons seeking recovery, it must provide daily, rather than once-weekly opportunities for communal worship, testimony and prayer, and it must challenge its parishioners to treat the church as their primary social community.[69]

He goes on to write: 'The overwhelming majority of addicts testify to the power of friendship as the single most important factor in their recoveries from addiction.'[70]

Aaron White, who works with drug abusers in Vancouver, also contends that addiction is caused by pain and dislocation and that there is therefore a need for addicted people to be connected to a loving community. He writes:

> Listening and committing are two of the most important tools we have when addressing addiction, and two of the most underused… we are convinced that meeting real brokenness

68 Dunnington, *Addiction and Virtue*, 190.

69 Dunnington, *Addiction and Virtue*, 191.

70 Dunnington, *Addiction and Virtue*, 185.

> with the real love and presence of Jesus is the true work of recovery, pastoral care, and Christian community.[71]

Some reading this might think, 'Well, I don't have time to meet with someone every day. I work full time, I have a family, as well as church commitments. Also, I have no clue about addictions – shouldn't they just attend a recovery group?'

The first comment is a valid one on one level. We only have a finite amount of time and some of us have busy jobs and lives. Family is important. However, a church that is seeking to disciple one another intentionally can find creative ways to do daily discipleship. Maybe you set up a WhatsApp group where people post what they've been learning each day. Maybe the membership set up a rota and have new Christians round to their houses a couple of times a week. Maybe you invite a newly converted person who has struggled with addiction to live with you. Maybe you invite this new Christian and their family on holiday with you and the family. We all have time on our hands and resources, it's just being intentional about how we use them and how we include others in it. This might mean we have to sacrifice some 'me' time and spend time with a new Christian – but ultimately it's worth it.

At Niddrie the church is open every day for prayer and as a staff we (including the pastor, the youth worker and the new Christian who is trying to keep busy) meet daily to pray and study the Bible. This means there is a connection point each day for anyone who wants it.

The second comment – shouldn't they just go to a recovery group – is something that I hear a lot. My response

71 White, *Recovering*, 26, 28.

is that recovery groups can be helpful if they are run in a way that integrates new believers into the life of the local church.

However, there are two big dangers to 'recovery' groups. The first is that recovery groups can just end up being a collection of people from similar backgrounds who are cut off from the rest of the church. The beauty of the church is that we spend time with people who are *like us* and *not like us*. The addict needs that as much as any other believer. The church is the central means by which a believer grows as the Word is preached and as the Christian loves those who are from different backgrounds.

A second danger of recovery groups is that they can produce a group of people who are simply looking to the past and glorifying their addictions. People have similar narratives and that can produce 'spiritual narcissism' where the self is elevated.[72]

Mercadante helpfully writes: 'Small groups are social forms. They can mediate God's grace, but they can just as easily promote their own interests and survival. They can become too inward looking, resistant to criticism, and unwilling to question their deepest presuppositions and structures.'[73] The recovery movement can become self-absorbed and end up producing a clique. They can slip into talking just about the past instead of the present.

However, the local church, focused on the grace of God, brings together people from a variety of backgrounds who in turn show the world the love of Jesus Christ (John 13:34, 1 John 4:7–8). The person who has struggled with addiction in their past will grow to consider others' needs above their

72 Mercadante, *Victims and Sinners,* 178.

73 Mercadante, *Victims and Sinners*, 178.

own when they have been humbled by the cross of Christ and are serving people who are very different from them.

Finally, the whole concept of recovery is not a biblical concept. We don't 'recover' from addictions. No, the Bible says we are new creations and, as men and women filled with the Spirit, we put to death the deeds of the flesh and walk in step with the Holy Spirit. Addictions – like any other sinful habits – need to die.

At Niddrie we have a group that one of our members set up called Progressing Pilgrims. It's run on a Friday night – a night where temptation runs high. The group is open to all and holds out the word of life to all who attend. They pray, sing, preach the Bible and then have a time where they ask questions and share about their lives. Benny, who set the group up, repeats every week that the group is not a 'recovery group' but a 'discovery group.' They are discovering the depths of their sinful hearts while running to Christ for help. It keeps the gospel central.

Stevie, whose story we heard earlier, said this about life in church: 'Church has become a family and spiritual home where I am supported and cared for. People have been there for me when it's been good and bad.' This is key.

The power of boundaries and discipline

As Christians we need boundaries and accountability. Hebrews 3:12–14 instructs us to exhort one another so that we might not be hardened by sin's deceitfulness. In other words, we need one another because we are often blind to our own blindness. We think we see ourselves accurately, but we don't. We need others to help us see our blind spots so that we might grow in grace. Being in a local church helps provide that exhortation so that we might grow.

That is what the person struggling with addiction needs. During the time they've battled with their addiction, they've had no accountability and no boundaries. Addicts therefore are entitled, selfish and spoilt. They are like children who have been given what they want without any discipline. The church though provides people who will exhort the new believer so that they can grow as a Christian. Like a child, they need people to say no to them and maintain biblical boundaries.

And when the addict refuses to listen and continues in their sin then they need loving discipline to show them that their behaviour does not honour the Lord.

Church discipline is a vital ministry for two big reasons for the addict. First, it's vital so that we might protect the glory of Christ. We are new creations as Christians, but we still battle with our old habits (Gal. 5:17). And so, discipline is about correcting sin for the purpose of ensuring that church members are representing Jesus rightly. It's about calling Christians to be what they are called to be. We want to protect the witness of the church and the purity of the gospel of Jesus Christ. And when someone is not living in line with their profession, we challenge that so that they do not bring the gospel into disrepute.

This is important in the schemes where we live in such tight communities. Anything that happens is broadcast on Facebook and spread round the community like wildfire. It's not like a gathered church where people travel in, sometimes from a distance, meaning that we can keep things under wraps and hide our little sins. Sin in a scheme is always public and so we must ensure that the community around us knows who's in and who's out. The football lads often ask about someone, 'Are they still with the church, because they've been up to all sorts?' and I can say that they're not because they are being silly. It protects our witness in the community.

The second reason we need discipline is because it's good for us and helps us to grow. Some people think it is unloving to have rules and discipline but that is just not true. We can see that in Hebrews 12. God disciplines those he loves so that they might produce a harvest of righteousness (verses 6 and 11). When we are disciplined in a loving manner it helps us to see our blind spots and grow in Christlikeness. This is similar to when we discipline our children. We don't discipline them simply to punish them but to train them and the motivation is one of love. They need discipline to grow. So do we.

And so, we need to teach our churches that discipline is important for the Christian life. We are not disciplining because we are being harsh, but because we love the Lord Jesus and want to see His people grow, including the person battling with addiction.

Do I need to send the addicted person to rehab?

Several men and women from our church have been sent to Christian rehabilitation centres. This has been helpful as it's allowed these new Christians to get away from the noise of their scheme and have some time to detox and reset. Like a computer with a virus, the new believer needs to have a total reboot of mind, heart and soul. Christian rehabilitation centres can help do this.

One of the weaknesses of rehabilitation centres, however, is what addicts do after they complete their programme. Christian rehab facilities often struggle to connect their graduates with a local church community, because the relationships aren't there. The churches themselves don't know what to do with guys coming away from addictions as they are not set up with a discipleship programme.

So, addicts come out of rehab into the concrete jungle and have little or no support and soon they are sucked back into their old world. In many instances, they go back on the drugs worse than before. In some cases, they tragically end up overdosing because their bodies are no longer used to the substances entering their bodies.

All in all, we've found the key to be a change of environment. For a decade, we ran our own discipleship house that was connected to our church. It was a small, family-run house that was forty minutes from our church and enabled men and women to get away from the noise of their environments and the temptations of the scheme while having fellowship throughout the week at the church.

But no discipleship programme is foolproof. If an addict wants to use, then they will use. They lie, cheat and steal to get what they want. Sadly, only a handful of those we've seen converted and discipled have gone on to be clean and live fruitful lives to the glory of the Lord. As Jesus tells us in the parable of the sower, we sow the seed and only one out of four of the seeds is fruitful. Therefore, many we work with will return to their vomit (Prov. 26:11). As Jesus says, 'For many are called, but few are chosen' (Matt. 22:14).

But every soul that is truly saved is worth it.

The power of discipleship

Finally, the local church helps disciple and train the person who has struggled with addiction so that they serve in the church and society at large. Too many men and women get saved and all they are used for is a sensational testimony.

They are never taught the Bible. They are never taught to walk the walk. They are never trusted with leadership roles.

The church is the place where people who have struggled with addiction can be changed and transformed by the Holy Spirit and used for the glory of God. Every person who gets saved has gifts and talents and those gifts and talents need to be used to build up the body of Christ. Their gifts need to be recognised and fanned into flames. The leader's role is to equip the saints for works of service (Eph. 4:12) and that includes the addict.

But this will take time and effort. It will not happen overnight. If addictions are sinful habits, then there needs to be a reformation of these habits. Habits – as we saw earlier – are the second-nature routines that structure our days and weeks. These need to be slowly changed, as the addict learns to put to death his or her sinful habits and grow in the habits of grace. Instead of meeting with their friends to shoot up heroin, they meet with other believers for fellowship. Instead of beginning the day with a joint, they read the Word of God. Instead of running to their addictions because they are stressed, they learn to pray.

This means that older Christians must come alongside the addict to 'urge them to be self-controlled' (Titus 2:6). They need to show them what it looks like to follow Jesus. They need to keep them accountable. They need to encourage them when suffering comes along. They need to love them consistently. Discipleship of the addict is a long-term commitment to love, lead and laugh with the former substance user.

In particular, addicts must be taught that life will get more difficult when they submit their lives to Christ. Before, they were able to medicate their pain. They were free to run away from their problems. They were in the grip of Satan. However, when an addict comes to Christ, they have to find comfort and peace in the Lord instead of their substance. They have to deal with stress in a new way: they can't simply run away from their problems but must take responsibility. And they now enter a war with the world, the flesh and the devil.

The Scriptures are clear that suffering is the core means to test the genuineness of one's faith (James 1:2–4). Maturity is fostered as one faces adversity and endures. However, addicts are professional escapologists. They escape the stresses of life through their addiction and so they fail to grow. The addicted person therefore has not dealt with stress without their chosen substance and so they stop learning and growing. Psychologists corroborate this and argue that the minute that a person starts an addiction is the minute that that person stops developing as a person. To quote Stevie once again: 'Many addicted people just don't grow up. They suffer with arrested development because addiction stunts growth.' Therefore, training and discipleship will take time and effort within the local church as the addict perseveres through trials and temptations.

One of the things we've learned at Niddrie is that for this to happen we need to let new believers stand on their own two feet. Often we can help people out of good intentions and end up hurting them because we over-help. We don't let new believers make their own mistakes. We over-disciple them. We end up making them dependent on us instead of the Lord Jesus Christ.

Conclusion

The local church is the best place to keep and grow the addict. The addicted person who has become a Christian is a new creation and they need nurturing through a healthy local church which teaches the Scriptures, has a healthy loving community, keeps them accountable and trains them to mature and grow as a disciple of Jesus Christ. May God help our churches be like the early church in Acts 2 where all believers – whether poor or rich, religious or irreligious – were welcome and devoted themselves to the teaching of God's Word, the breaking of bread and to prayer.

Kim's life is remarkably different from what it was five years ago. She has grown as a believer within the local church and is no longer addicted. She has cultivated healthy habits of prayer and reading God's Word. Her oldest child became a Christian and is now baptised at the church. She is training to be a gospel worker and serves faithfully within the local church. All praise to King Jesus!

Discussion Questions:

1. The chapter began by thinking of the importance of the local church – why do addicts need the local church? What are the weaknesses of having recovery groups that are separate from the local church?
2. Why is it important churches teach the whole counsel of God? Why do addicts need to feed on God's word more than anything else?
3. Why is genuine community important for all believers but particularly the addict? In what ways can your church grow relationally and include the broken in its everyday practices?
4. Why is church discipline important for all believers but particularly the addict? Why do we struggle

with discipline? Why is it loving? How does it help us grow?

5. Why does discipleship need to be long term with the addict?

6

TRAINING THE ADDICT

Mez McConnell

And he gave the apostles, the prophets, the evangelists, the shepherds and teachers, to equip the saints for the work of ministry, for building up the body of Christ, until we all attain to the unity of the faith and of the knowledge of the Son of God, to mature manhood...

—Paul (Eph. 4:11–13)

My name is Brian. I'm forty-four and I was raised in Greenock. My mum raised my three siblings and me on her own. We didn't have a lot, but I knew I was loved. I was painfully shy and always felt the need to belong to something and feel accepted. To begin with, this involved being the class clown, which resulted in getting into trouble in school and in the family home too.

I was quick to cling to anything that I felt gave me an identity or made me feel part of something. I first smoked cannabis and drank alcohol at the age of twelve or thirteen.

This got me into a lot of trouble at home, but I was willing to risk that because I felt accepted and part of something. By the age of seventeen, I was smoking heroin, because of which my life changed dramatically. By the age of nineteen, I was homeless, self-harming and in prison. This would be an on-and-off pattern for my life for most of the next nineteen to twenty years.

I entered Christian rehab (a place called the Haven) in early 2016 and fell in love with Christ on 25 April 2016. Leaving rehab and living independently was not easy and would have been a great deal harder on my own. I went to Edinburgh in January 2018 – to 20schemes. I volunteered there for a year as part of a team who were seeking to plant a church there. I was discipled by mature Christian men who were from similar and completely different backgrounds to me. What each had in common was a love for Christ, a love for me and a desire to see me grow in Christian maturity. Accountability was a huge part of this. Prior to this, many of the men who took an interest in what I was doing and how I was getting on were police officers investigating a crime I was suspected of. But I soon realised that a big part of growing in Christian maturity is not only being honest with and accountable to God, but being honest with and accountable to each other.

I'm now a gospel worker with Street Connect in Glasgow. I'm blessed to now be able to support and point others to Christ, showing them the love I was shown.

More than a trophy of grace!

I first heard the term 'trophy of grace' not long after I had been converted. I had been out of prison for about six months and I was trying my best to walk with Jesus. I had gone back to college and I had begun a ministry to my homeless friends in the community. I was attending my local church and I was being regularly discipled by one of the leaders. I was growing in the faith.

I was introduced to a visiting speaker one day and he suddenly exclaimed, 'What a trophy of grace you are!' I just smiled, completely clueless as to his meaning. When I asked my friend in private later, he shrugged and said it just meant the unexpected conversion of a person most people would have thought were beyond salvation. I didn't know whether to be offended or proud.

Years later, I would think back to that conversation, and think: 'All believers are trophies of grace. All believers are a miracle of new life. All believers are unexpected converts to everybody but God, who predestined them before they were even born!'

But I didn't know that then. Then, it meant that I was an oddity in Christian churches to such a degree that I was paraded around as some sort of mini-celebrity. The only thing I had done to earn my fame was come from a terrible background. I became the guy who got wheeled out at testimony nights and church evangelistic outreaches.

I was their trophy, but I wanted to do more than just sit on a pedestal and be admired. I wanted to learn more about how I could serve God with my whole life.

The dangerous sin of idleness

I soon got tired of the testimony bandwagon. I wanted to do something more with my new life. I wanted to really dig into the Bible. I wanted to study it every day, but people just didn't seem to have the time. They were just getting on with their lives while I felt trapped in a testimony time-warp.

I loved Sundays and I loved my weekly meeting with my mentor, but I had little structure the rest of the time.

I picked up the odd bit of work here and there, but nobody was going to employ an ex-con on parole. I had no discernible skills and the thought of working the factory floor in a low-challenge job filled me with dread and depression. Boredom began to strike and with it the temptation to go back to my old way of life.

I had lived my life without much personal discipline and it was beginning to show. Nobody at the church knew. Why would they? I was the trophy-of-grace guy and on nodding terms with about 99% of the congregation. But nobody really knew me and I didn't know them. We all seemed to love Jesus, but that was it.

It wasn't long before I got into a habit of staying up late at night playing video games and sleeping in until the afternoon. Slowly, but surely, I was becoming more and more depressed. I began to stop reading the Bible as I once had. My mind began to drift back to old friends in the town. I began to romanticise my old life. 'It wasn't that bad,' I told myself. 'Actually, most of it was a good laugh.'

It was all lies.

Thankfully, I shared my concerns with one of my Christian friends and he convinced me to go back to college and volunteer at a homeless charity in the town. Almost immediately, my mood changed as I got stuck into the work. I excelled at the studies and had a real passion for the homeless work. I got back into the Bible and began to find church enjoyable again. I was beginning to build some sort of structure and purpose in my life and it felt good after years of drug dealing, prison and sofa surfing.

It is true what Richard Baxter once said:

> Idleness is the mother and nurse of many heinous sins. They that do not what they should, will be doing what they should not. Idleness is the season of temptation. It is Satan's seedtime. It is then that he has opportunity to tempt men to malice, revenge, and all other villainy that is committed.[74]

This is one of the main motivations behind the set-up of Niddrie Community and 20schemes. Many of the people we evangelise come from chaotic backgrounds. Many didn't finish high school, or they were regularly absent. Many haven't held a normal job for years. Many have never worked. And then they come to faith in Christ and everything changes.

What do they do now? What will they do with their days now that they aren't getting high and wasting their lives? Can the church help them? Should the church help them? In response to these questions, we developed our own special internship programmes.

20schemes church internships

We operate them at our churches in 20schemes for two main reasons:

- For personal discipline and training for future mission in the workplace
- For personal discipline and future vocational ministry training[75]

---

74 Quoted in Keith Christensen, 'Counseling Idleness', Association of Certified Biblical Counselors, 10 March 2021, https://biblicalcounseling.com/resource-library/conference-messages/counseling-idleness/.

75 Not all of the churches in our network operate in exactly the same way.

Discipline is the key word. We are preparing all of our new believers for service in the kingdom, whether they go on to plant a church or work on the bin lorries. All is to be done for the glory of God. Discipline works. It is our experience in partnership with a local rehab centre that almost all of the men who finish their year-long programme with us will persevere in the faith once they leave. They finish it having completed an intense discipleship programme and having developed a strong and disciplined work ethic.

Our internship programme is a combination of Bible study and some form of manual labour or other voluntary service. We have found that putting people to work early on in their faith has great spiritual benefit for them in the long-term. The more we can fill their time with physical work and spiritual reflection, the less time they have to get into trouble.

Brandon Crowe maintains that:

> ... doing something constructive often leads us away from temptation, especially when that something is focused on and consistent with biblical truths. If nature abhors a vacuum, so do our hearts: if we are not filling our hearts with positive, biblical truths – and engaging in positive, biblical activities – our sinful hearts are prone to leading us in destructive, unbiblical directions (which tend to be in keeping with the world's standards).[76]

The antidote to idleness is work and purposeful activity. That's what we seek to offer in our internships, a mixture of Bible study, discipline and honest work. Spurgeon says this about idleness: 'Some temptations come to the industrious,

76 Brandon D. Crowe, 'Idleness and Temptation', *Table Talk*, January 2022, https://tabletalkmagazine.com/article/2022/01/idleness-and-temptation/.

but *all* temptations attack the idle.'[77] When our people are focused on something other than themselves, it gives the enemy less chance to come in and play havoc with their minds. Work is a *good* thing, not bad. And every Christian has been saved to serve. The job of all pastors is to prepare their people for works of service. Our job, then, is to find out what those works of service are for each soul under our care. Richard Baxter has said:

> He that has some physical or mental weariness from a physical condition or a calm stoic temperament, a heaviness, or a dullness, still does sin if he strives not against it as much as he can, and as in reason he should. He is most sinfully slothful who is most voluntarily slothful. As he that endeavours least against it, and he that loves it most and would not leave it: and he that is least troubled at it and least repents and laments it and contrives to accommodate his sloth.[78]

Spiritual accountability

Addicts tend to be very emotional people and they can make bad decisions on the spur of the moment. This is often a harder habit to break than whatever it is they are addicted to. They need some mature wise voices speaking into their lives. They need some accountability, otherwise they will soon fall back into old patterns of thinking and behaving. This accountability is a key part of our training and discipleship.

---

77 Charles H. Spurgeon on 'Idleness' from *Gleanings Among the Sheaves*, 2nd edition (Sheldon & Company, 1869), available at https://www.gutenberg.org/files/42657/42657-h/42657-h.htm

78 Quoted in Christensen, 'Counseling Idleness'.

At Niddrie, we give everybody a mentor so that they can have somebody to turn to when things begin to get on top of them. They need someone with whom they can be totally honest about their temptations and their failures. One of Satan's most popular tricks is to isolate believers and make them think that nobody understands them, or that they're not good enough for Jesus. When that happens, we need to hear the wisdom of a mature believer who can encourage us, rebuke us, and pray for and with us.

In Galatians 6:1–2, every church member is encouraged to participate in one another's spiritual lives and soul care. Sometimes that means calling out sin; at other times it may mean challenging an errant brother or sister. In James 5:16 we are explicitly called to confess our sins to one another so that we may receive prayer and healing. Both of these texts assume a degree of mutual vulnerability and spiritual love within the body of Christ.

> Brothers, if anyone is caught in any transgression, you who are spiritual should restore him in a spirit of gentleness. Keep watch on yourself, lest you too be tempted. Bear one another's burdens, and so fulfil the law of Christ. (Gal. 6:1–2)

> Therefore, confess your sins to one another and pray for one another, that you may be healed. The prayer of a righteous person has great power as it is working. (James 5:16)

Helping the families of addicts

Spouses, partners, children and other family members are often the unseen victims of addicts. They've had to put up with their lies, manipulation, violence, theft and all sorts of abuse, usually over many years. They are usually broken mentally and physically by what they've been put through.

Therefore, we must be careful when making an ex-addicted convert a minor celebrity in our churches. They have often left a trail of devastation in their wake that needs to be dealt with as part of their ongoing discipleship process. While it is true that God forgives their sins and remembers them no more (Heb. 8:12), there are still the consequences of it that they need to face up to.

Part of our ministry as the local church should be to reach out to affected family members and to explain to them what is going on in the soul of their loved – or not so loved – one. Many family members get angry when the addict returns home to proclaim that all his sins have been paid for by Christ. They think that this means that what the addict has done to them over many years has now been forgiven and forgotten. While that may be true in the heavens, on earth it is not the case.

It will take months, and even years, of gentle counsel to help the true victims of an addict's abusive past. Some of them may never forgive him or her, and they will have to live with that. The best he can do in that situation is seek their forgiveness and keep praying to the Lord that one day they may be reconciled.

I always tell those I pastor that what took years for someone to destroy and abuse is not going to be solved overnight. The abused spouse is not going to love them overnight because they've found the Lord. It is going to take a lot of time, patience and prayer. The most important thing the ex-addict can do is to walk closely to Jesus and win others over by consistently walking in the power of the Holy Spirit.

They won't be won by promises that someone has changed. They've heard it all before. But in my experience, they *are* won over by seeing a new consistent lifestyle far removed from the old one. They are won over when they see that their family member has forsaken all of his old friends and haunts and is now committed to God's people in the local church.

Of course, some family members and friends will dismiss the conversion as nothing more than a fad or some form of brain washing. But, with the support and encouragement of God's people, even the pain of this can be lessened.

At Niddrie, we have provided counselling for family members, housing, financial support and even holidays for children affected by addiction. There are a hundred and one things the local church can do if we put our minds to it.

Conclusion

Reaching addicts with the gospel is only the start of a lifelong process of discipleship. That discipleship and training is best served in the local church. Most ex-addicts are accustomed to receiving not giving. They lack discipline unless it is in the pursuit of drink or drugs. They are easily tempted into the sin of idleness which, in turn, puts them at risk from Satan's fiery darts.

They need to know what true Christianity looks like lived out and they need to see it operating within a local body of believers. They need to take their place in the church and learn to be servants not just recipients. The church should be able to offer voluntary jobs and an intense teaching programme to help reintegrate these new believers into society.

We want to make disciples who will make a valuable, God-honouring, contribution to a society they've long abused and taken so much from. We want to be preparing missionaries for the workplace and even for vocational roles within the church itself.

Discussion Questions:

1. More than a trophy of grace – how can the term trophy of grace hinder the work of discipleship with the addict?
2. How does idleness kill the Christian? Are there ways that your church can better train/disciple those struggling with addictions? Do you have a discipleship pathway for addicts?
3. Why is it important to help the families of those who have struggled with addictions? What do you think that looks like?

7

PERSEVERING WITH THE ADDICT

Andy Constable

There's a refuge for every lustful thought
From old habits enticing me away
When I fear my addictions won't be overcome
There is hope through Christ's resurrection day
—Sol Fenne, 'Flee From Sin (Run To Jesus)'[79]

Don't let your emotional life be controlled by the sin you see in others.
—Jack Miller[80]

'Jimmy has bolted [run away] and he's not picking up his phone,' said the manager of our discipleship house on the phone. Jimmy is a recent convert from our scheme. He has struggled with alcohol and drugs since the age of eleven, but he has recently heard the gospel, been convicted of his sins and trusted in Jesus. Due to the temptations that he faces

79 Sol Fenne, *Flee From Sin (Run To Jesus)*, 2018. Quoted with permission.

80 Jack Miller, *The Heart of a Servant Leader* (P&R Publishing, 2004), 133..

in our community, we moved him into our discipleship house for some intensive discipleship. We have spent many hours of time investing in his life. We have spent a lot of money covering travel and food costs. He has been baptised and become a member. He has become part of the church family. But now he has run back to his addiction. What should we do?

This is a typical story. We invest our time and energy into people and then, out of nowhere, it blows up in our faces. We don't know what to do. Do we chase them and get them back? What do we say when we see them? Do we chastise them or hug them? Do we need to move through our discipline process? When is the time to remove them from membership?

Discipleship is a painful and bloody road. The Lord Jesus said it would be this way. 'If anyone would come after me,' He said, 'let him deny himself and take up his cross daily and follow me' (Luke 9:23). The cross was a place of horror in the ancient world. A brutal and barbaric way to die. And Jesus was saying that's what it would mean for His disciples to follow Him. They would have to put to death their own way of living and live wholeheartedly for their Saviour – sacrificing their very own lives to follow Him. The problem – the old self doesn't die easily (Col. 3:5). Our sinful habits can become so engrained that they are difficult to change. Our love has been attuned to the songs of this world and so it takes time to adjust the radio frequency. Our addictions cling so closely that they are a shadow that constantly overcomes us.

For this reason, discipleship of an addict is going to be a long, bloody road. It's going to take perseverance. The discipler needs to be ready for the long haul. For the marathon. For the ups and downs of the addict's life. It's not going to be easy. But Jesus never said it would be. The letters of the New Testament all attest to new believers fighting, struggling, battling with sin, believing false doctrines and being wooed by the world. Like it was back then, so it is now for every believer.

Setbacks

It is important to understand that although the power of sin is broken in an addict's life, there is still the pollution of sin whirling inside their souls. They have entered into a spiritual battle against the world, the flesh and the devil. And so there are going to be setbacks along the way. They are not going to be the finished article from day one. The Christian life is a process of sanctification where each person grows in holiness till the day of Christ Jesus.

This is a daily war.

What I've found as I've discipled men and women from backgrounds of addictions is that there are a number of phases they go through. The first phase (the honeymoon) in their Christian journey is getting converted. At this point everything is exciting. They feel the relief of their sins being removed from them. They are overwhelmed by the goodness of God. They can't believe that Christ loves them and died for them. They are literally skipping down the streets with a spring in their step, sharing the good news with friends and family.

The second phase to their Christian journey is dealing with temptation. They've been a Christian for a few weeks. They've managed to stay away from old friends. They've stayed clean off the drugs and said no to the temptations that are around them. They try to cut down on their methadone. However, the shine begins to wear off. They come under attack from their friends and family for being one of those 'Bible bashers'. They realise that they don't have as much money as they used to have. They miss the buzz of going out at the weekend and having a couple of pints with the lads. They begin to dibble dabble again. A little bit here, a little bit there. They try to walk with Christ but feel this new sense of guilt. They realise that the Christian walk is not for the fainthearted.

The third phase is hitting the wall. The shine has worn off completely and the honeymoon phase is long gone. The temptations have built up in their heads and a plan begins to form about how they can get out of the 'straight jacket' of following Jesus. They long for their old lives like the people of Israel who gazed back at slavery in Egypt from the wilderness. They keep their heads down during the week and plan to get their fix at the weekend. They lie about their whereabouts, turn off their phones and sink the pint which leads to coke and a whole weekend of so-called pleasure. The bender can last a weekend or sometimes weeks. You wonder where they are and what they are up to – they are knee-deep in sin.

The fourth phase is coming to their senses. After the last stage, if they are saved, they usually return with their tail between their legs, feeling the shame and guilt of their sins. They realise that their addictions are a waste of time and get them nowhere. At this point, their hearts are teachable. If the Spirit of the Lord is within them, then they listen to your advice and you can point them towards Jesus. The return is always a difficult time. It's important to discern whether a person is truly repentant or just feeling self-pity. It's important to help them think through what proper repentance looks like and for them to lift their eyes to Calvary. Self-pity is not a sign of godliness. Taking responsibility for their own sin is crucial here.

The final phase is growth. If they belong to the Lord then they will learn from their mistakes. They will admit their sin and seek accountability and help. They will take responsibility for their actions and put in place a battle plan to grow in Christ. This is where we as disciplers can keep them accountable and point them to Christ.

And then… the cycle can happen *again*!

This is the way of many who struggle with addiction.

Some people will kick their addictions straight away and never return to them – but these stories are few and far between. For most it's a story of ups and downs. One step forward. Three steps back. Heartache. Hurt. A battle.

As Kevin De Young puts it, 'We like our sins and dying to them is painful. Almost everything is easier than growing in godliness. So, we try and fail, try and fail, and then give up.'[81]

The key for you if you are discipling an addict is that you must expect setbacks. You must expect heartache. It's not going to be plain sailing. But don't be alarmed. Instead, be prepared.

Early signs

I still remember the first time this pattern happened to me. A man moved in with my family straight from prison. He had struggled with drugs and ended up serving time. However, a minister went to visit him in prison and ended up sharing the gospel with him. He repented of his sins and trusted in Christ. The problem was that he needed to get out of the city that he lived in. There were too many temptations, so he ended up coming to me.

---

81 Kevin De Young, *The Hole in our Holiness* (Crossway, 2012), 19.

We accepted this man into our family. He ate with us. He lived with us. He joined our church. We invested hours of time into the relationship.

But then one day he bolted back to the city he came from. He turned off his phone. And he didn't come back. I was devastated. I couldn't sleep for days after it. I was angry: how could he do this after all we've done for him? I was sad: had we done something wrong? What's he going to do now? I was confused: where was God in this? I thought he wanted to follow the Lord. I was depressed: what am I going to do now? It feels like ministry is a waste of time.

I should have seen it coming. The signs were all there. He was distancing himself from me. He was coming back from weekend visits to see his son later and later. He smelt of alcohol at different times and looked bleary eyed. He started to cut corners at work. His head seemed to be somewhere else. But I ignored it, thinking that he was just going through a tough season.

And then he upped and left.

So how do we persevere with the addict in these situations? What do we do when they walk away? What do we do if they are at it and then come back again? How do we disciple people when they are constantly stumbling and tripping as they walk the narrow path?

Be prepared

When the lad who had stayed with us walked away from the Lord, I wasn't prepared. I had read the glamorous stories of those who had worked with addicts and the testimonies where people left their addictions behind completely never to return to them again. However, that is not the reality in many cases. For many they will stumble, trip, and fall, time and time again. They will get sober, walk with the Lord, get a job, and then run back to their addictions again, lose it all, and have to start again. This is the reality of addiction and sanctification. It is slow. It does not happen in a straight line. It's victory and loss. Trust and witness can be lost in one weekend. But we know that those who belong to the Lord will persevere because they have the Spirit living inside of them, drawing them back to the Lord and His holy church.

One of our church members – Stevie, who you met earlier on in the book – made a commitment to follow Christ ten years ago. He has been through this cycle time and time again. It's been a painful and costly journey for him. He has had months of complete sobriety and then starts to dibble dabble in the old life and then completely crash and burn. However, he keeps coming back in repentance. The Lord keeps bringing him back. The Lord keeps working in his life.

Again, that is no different from any other Christian. Think for a minute about your own life. How often have you been proud and ignored godly advice in your life? How many times have you been selfish with your time and resources instead of being generous and open handed? How often have you been impatient in the house and yelled at the kids because they have got in the way of what you want? What about the last time you lusted after someone who is not your spouse? What about your lack of faith? The list goes on.

The difference between someone who is saved and not saved is not the presence of sin in a person's life, but this – are they repenting and growing and moving forward? Do they confess their sin when they mess up and return to the Lord?

As pastoral carers we must remember that discipleship will be messy with the addict. They are bringing their chaos with them. So be prepared. Trust the Lord.

Parable of the sower

One of the parables that has helped me most as I've worked with those who struggle with addictions is the parable of the sower. The parable is told by Jesus in Matthew 13, Mark 4 and Luke 8. The parable is a simple one. A sower goes out to sow seed. As he sows the seed, some of it falls along the path and birds eat it up. Other seeds fall on rocky ground where there is little soil so it cannot take root and it's scorched by the sun. Other seeds fall among the thorns and are choked. And some seed falls on good, rich soil and produces a harvest.

The Lord Jesus explains that the seed is the Word of God and the soils are the different ways that people respond to the Word. Some will hear the Word and Satan will snatch that seed away from their hard hearts. Some will hear the Word, respond to it with joy, but then difficult times come their way and they decide that following Jesus is not for them. Still others will hear the Word and respond, but then the cares of the world tempt them away. And then some seed falls on rich soil and produces a bountiful spiritual crop.

This parable helps explain ministry in general but also with those struggling with addictions. Many addicts will hear the word of the gospel and simply ignore it. They will cling to their addictions and never let go. That is like the seed that's snatched away by the devil. He doesn't want them to see light and life and freedom. He wants them to remain blind, battered and broken by their addictions. Many addicts will hear the gospel and respond with great joy. They will give up their addiction for a season and follow

Jesus. They will be filled with joy. They will tell others about this wonderful news. And then a bit of suffering comes, or a bit of persecution or a hard decision, and they wander back to their addictions. The genuineness of their faith is tested and they falter.

And then you have some seed that falls on good soil. People hear the gospel and their hearts are changed and they become fruitful in the kingdom. Now that's not to say it's all plain sailing, as we have seen. However, slowly but surely, they throw off the shackles of their addictions and enjoy the freedom won for them in Christ.

The key for the sower here is to be faithful. Sometimes we can look at the people we've shared the gospel with, especially those who have struggled with addictions, and wonder if we have done something wrong? Why have so many walked away from the faith? Why have so many gone to addiction centres, professed faith, got clean and then walked straight back to their addictions afterwards? Why have others flourished? This parable helps us answer those questions. But is also reminds us to keep going.

Don't get hard-hearted

One of the greatest enemies when one works with those battling with addictions is hard-heartedness. It is easy to become cynical in response to being lied to again and again and again. But hard-heartedness will kill your love for people and will cause you to doubt the power of the gospel. Yes, we should grow in healthy discernment where we understand that cycles of deception, manipulation and addiction don't die easily. Like Jesus, we don't entrust ourselves to men because we know what it is in man (John 2:24–25) – we are all sinners at the end of the day. But we need to keep soft hearts where we are willing to give men and women another chance despite their lies, and put our trust in the Lord who can work a miracle of grace in any person.

So how do we keep those soft hearts and persevere with the addict?

First, we pray. This seems like a nice *Christian* answer, but it's the most important thing we can do. We need to commit those we are discipling constantly to the Lord. The temptations of the flesh and the attacks of the enemy are constantly at the heels of young believers. It's only the Lord, if indeed they are saved, who can help the young believer grow in grace. And if the Spirit of God is living in them, then He will constantly carry them home to their church family if they have walked back to their addictions.

Our first instinct, especially when someone bolts, is to chase after them. We text. We ring. We run around the scheme looking for them. But, if someone wants to contact you then they will. Don't panic. Don't get overwhelmed by the situation. Don't think that your whole church is going to fall because your trophy of grace has done a runner. Entrust their souls to the Lord.

Second, watch your own heart. Often our first reaction to someone's sin is self-righteousness. How could they be so stupid? How dare they? Often, our self-righteousness quickly becomes a hardening of our heart towards them. This particularly happens when it's a repeated pattern in a person's life. When they do the same stupid thing again and again, we start to harbour bitterness, resentment and anger towards them. How dare they waste our time? What about all the things we did for them? This is a real danger.

When someone walks away from the church, we need to think about the people of Israel in the Old Testament or the disciples with Jesus. We need to remember how the people of Israel walked away from the Lord so many times, and yet how gracious the Lord was with them. Or how the disciples just didn't understand who Jesus was initially, despite the many miracles He performed. And yet how patient He was with them.

When Peter asked Jesus how many times he should forgive his brother, Jesus answered him by saying, '*seven times seventy-seven*' (Matt. 18:21–35, emphasis added). In other words, time and time and time and time and time and time again. Many of our men and women fall hard, and publicly, but this is not a time for self-righteous judgementalism. Instead, we ought to assess our own hearts and remember the grace we have been shown many times by the Lord.

Mature believers who are not bathed in the gospel often run to self-righteousness because they are not getting drunk or taking drugs. But an addict walking back to their public folly is no worse than us keeping our private little sins locked away behind closed doors. We are all damned sinners who are saved by grace. When we remember that, it helps us to keep a soft heart towards those we are discipling after a fall.

Third, counsel the gospel. Many of our members who are saved from our community are like boomerangs – they come back at some point. It's not like in a gathered church where people can run off to another part of the city and avoid Christians for years on end. We are a closed community and we will inevitably see the person who has chosen sin. Our people often come back to see us when they are ready. The key, if they are repentant, is to counsel the gospel.

We need to remind them that their sin is against the Lord, not us. We need to remind them that they need to repent and not wallow in self-pity. And we need to point them ultimately to Jesus and his death on the cross.

A favourite set of verses I read during an initial meeting like this is 1 John 1:5–10:

> This is the message we have heard from him and proclaim to you, that God is light, and in him is no darkness at all. If we say we have fellowship with him while we walk in darkness, we lie and do not practice the truth. But if we walk in the light, as he is in the light, we have fellowship with one another, and the blood of Jesus his Son cleanses us from all sin. If we say we have no sin, we deceive ourselves, and the truth is not in us. If we confess our sins, he is faithful and just to forgive us our sins and to cleanse us from all unrighteousness. If we say we have not sinned, we make him a liar, and his word is not in us.

These verses remind us that we are *all* sinners and that if we deny it, then we deny the gospel. They remind us of our need to walk in the light, not the darkness. And they remind us to confess our sins and Jesus will cleanse us from *all* unrighteousness.

The problem with many Christians (and I've been one of them) is that they counsel legalism. We say, 'If you just do x, y and z then things will be better.' Give up your phone. Stop watching TV. Read your Bible more. Cut down on your methadone. But the reality is that in giving rules to a rule-breaker, we are giving them an open invitation to just break them again! The only person who can help someone beat their addictions is Jesus. There is power in only one place and that's in the finished work of Jesus. We need to point them to Jesus and the glorious fact that, 'Our sins they are many, his mercy is more.'[82]

---

82 Matt Boswell, Matt Papa, 'His Mercy Is More', (Getty Music Hymns and Songs; Getty Music Publishing; Love Your Enemies Publishing; Messenger Hymns, 2016).

Now that's not to say that we don't suggest some immediate measures, such as handing over their bank card or phones. Sometimes we need to put them in a safe place to remove temptations. But we don't leave them with that. We can take phones, money and even move them to the middle of the desert, but they will still find somewhere to get drunk and shoot up again if they want to. They need to see the stupidity and darkness of sin, the beauty of Christ, that true contentment is only found in Him.

The fourth way to keep a soft heart while persevering with the addict is this: if there are no signs of repentance over a prolonged period then you move through the *discipline* process. We move through slowly and patiently according to Matthew 18. As we thought earlier, boundaries are important. Just as they help children understand what is right and wrong and grow into healthy, mature adults, they help the addict to know that their actions will be held to account – and this will help them grow.

Finally, trust the Lord and keep pressing on! Ministry in any situation is brutal. It's not for the faint hearted. If you are going to keep a soft heart and persevere with the addict then you need to remember that God is in control and you are not. Remember that He is the one who saves. He is the one who sanctifies. He is the one who holds the believer fast. And He is the one who is working out all things for the good of those who love Him. A healthy understanding of God's sovereignty will help you to persevere because you will remember that you are not God and so you will keep trusting in His good and perfect purposes.

Mez often counsels me after a setback in ministry – pray for them, trust the Lord, enjoy the blessings you have in front of you and keep pressing on. At the end of the day, you cannot control people and their decisions – all you can do is be a faithful disciple who points people to the Lord and leave the rest in His hands.

Conclusion

Every person who seeks to disciple someone from a background of addiction will need perseverance. This is one of the hallmarks of the Christian faith – perseverance and endurance. As disciplers you must be ready for it – those you are discipling are babies in the faith and there are many dangers ahead. Like a parent you will have to be there in the ups and downs of life, constantly warning them of the dangers of sin, picking them up when they fall, and including them in your lives even when you feel like you don't want to anymore. It is important to cultivate discernment alongside a soft and tender heart that is bathed in the gospel and trusting in God's good and perfect purposes. The Lord Jesus said, 'I will build my church, and the gates of hell shall not prevail against it.'

Press on!

Discussion Questions:

1. Why do we need to persevere with the addict?
2. Have you ever experienced the cycle of someone you have discipled upping and leaving, returning to the vomit of their addictions? How did it feel? How did you respond?
3. Read the Parable of the Sower from the gospels: how does this help us understand why some return to their old patterns of life? How does this encourage you in your ministry?
4. How do we maintain a tender and discerning heart towards those we are discipling from addictive backgrounds?

8

THE FINAL WORD

Hoping in Christ

Andy Constable

Addictions are simple on many levels, as we have seen – they are sinful patterns of behaviour that enslave and destroy a person. They promise the fleeting pleasures of this world but leave a person spiritually hungry. They promise life but in fact bring death. They cover pain for a time but leave a person with unresolved issues that cripple them, leaving them unable to cope with the stresses of life. The addict rebels against God and the world. Like the rest of humanity, the addict is a pitiable sinner.

Therefore, at one level, the answer to the problem of addiction is easy: the addict needs the gospel of the Lord Jesus Christ. The apostle Paul writes, 'I am not ashamed of the gospel because it is the power of salvation for everyone who believes' (Rom. 1:16). The precious gospel that Jesus lived, died, rose again, and is ascended forevermore for pitiable sinners is the only message that can truly save a soul and therefore change a person's life. The gospel therefore needs to be central when we minister to anyone – including the addict. If we depart from the gospel, then we are communicating that the addict needs saving in a different way to everybody else. We are implying that the Lord Jesus is unable to break the chains of addiction and replace the heart of stone with a heart of flesh.

However, addictions are also complex. The habits formed by addictions are all-encompassing, affecting mind, body and soul. Addictions hit the reward pathways which simply means they are hard to say no to. Addictions are often masking pain and suffering which means, when they are removed, the addict has a whole load of unresolved pain and stress to deal with. Addictions destroy a person but give meaning and purpose at the same time.

So as we end we just want to give a word to churches, recovery groups, and anyone reading this book struggling with addictions. For each group we want to end with some questions for you to think through as you think about how to apply what you have learned (if anything) from this book.

Local Churches

As we have contended throughout the book the church is central in God's plans to reach the world. It is the bride of Christ (Eph. 5:25) and the central mechanism for discipling the believer whatever their background including the addict. It is important for local churches to therefore think through two things.

First, if you are a local church, then you may like to consider how you can reach the addict and disciple and train them for works of service more effectively. Maybe you are only using your new Christians for testimonies, instead of giving them real responsibilities? Are you living open and vulnerable lives that provide real community, welcoming the addict and enabling them to open up about their battles and struggles? We hope this book has helped you think through your church culture.

Planting local churches

Second, it is important that churches seek to plant churches in poorer communities. If the gospel is what saves a soul and the local church is what best displays the gospel then we need to plant more churches. In the UK we need to rethink how we are reaching the addict. Recovery groups serve a purpose, often giving a safe place to those battling with their addictions. However, poorer communities need healthy local churches. The local church can offer the long-term support and discipleship the addict needs. The local church can provide the boundaries that the addict has missed throughout their lives to help them mature. The local church holds out the word of life which helps the addict grow. The local church provides a family of people who are like the addict and not like the addict so that by their love for one another the world can see that they are the Lord Jesus' disciples.

Recovery Groups

If you are a recovery group or rehabilitation centre, we want to encourage you that the work you are doing is important and necessary. You are working with men and women who have been on the edge of hopelessness and death, and God uses you powerfully to give them the hope of the gospel, life in Jesus' name and ongoing care and discipleship. However, you may wish to take the opportunity to rethink your discipleship and how you are getting your people involved with local churches after reading this book. Use your experience to strengthen churches so they can better serve those you are seeking to minister to. Recovery groups and rehabs should exist to work alongside and with local churches, not replace them.

Here are some questions to consider: In your discipleship are you teaching the addict about the importance and necessity of the local church? Are your workers/employees involved in solid gospel churches in order to be examples to your clients? Do you have a network of churches who will care for those struggling with addictions after they've finished their rehab program? If you are a recovery group are you teaching God's word and helping people integrate themselves into the life of a local church? Are you meeting with church leaders in order to help them understand addictions and how to care for those in the throes of addiction? Again, it is vital that rehabs and recovery groups build up the local church and help those struggling with addictions to find a home there for their good and God's glory.

Addict

To the addict who feels like they won't amount to anything – know that there is hope in the gospel of the Lord Jesus Christ. He came to seek and save that which was lost. He came to die for sinners who have made a mess of their lives. He did not come for the healthy but the sick. And He can change any person's life and give them a new direction. The testimonies throughout the book testify to the saving grace of the Lord Jesus Christ. He alone can piece back together a life broken by addiction. Nobody is too lost, nobody is too sinful, nobody is too broken for the Lord Jesus Christ.

But make sure you find a good, solid, Bible-believing church that will nurture you and disciple you. Do not despise the church and its funny quirks but immerse yourself in a local church. Maybe you are currently only spending time with people who have had a similar background to you – well, we encourage you to burst out of the clique and learn from those who are different from you. Maybe you are battling with your addiction and life is up and down – we encourage you to keep going holding fast to the word of life while being supported by brothers and sisters from the church. Overall…

Keep going, trusting in the power of the gospel. All glory be to God!

RESOURCES

On Addiction:

Kent Dunnington, *Addiction and Virtue: Beyond the Models of Disease and Choice,* IVP Academic: 2011.

James K.A. Smith, *You Are What You Love: The Spiritual Power of Habit,* Brazos Press: 2016.

Mark Shaw, *The Heart of Addiction: A Biblical Perspective,* Focus Publishing: 2008.

Edward T. Welch, *Addictions: A Banquet in the Grave,* P&R Publishing: 2001.

Gabor Matè, *In the Realm of Hungry Ghosts: Close encounters with addiction*, Vermillion: 2018.

Caring for the Addict:

Emlet, Overcoming Addictions, BCUK Conference: https://www.biblicalcounselling.org.uk/video/overcoming-addiction/

Edward T. Welch, *Crossroads: A Step-By-Step Guide Away from Addiction Study Guide,* November: 2008.

Mez McConnell, ed., *First Steps Box Set,* Christian Focus Publishing: 2020.

Mez McConnell & Mike McKinley, *Church in Hard Place: How the Local Church Brings Life to the Poor and Needy,* Crossway: 2016.

Rosaria Butterfield, *The Gospel Comes with a House Key: Practicing Radically Ordinary Hospitality in Our Post-Christian World,* Crossway: 2018.

Mark Dever, *Discipling,* Crossway: 2016.

Helen Thorne & Steve Midgley, *Mental Health and your Church: A Handbook for Biblical Care,* The Good Book Company: 2023.

Also avilable from Mez McConnell ...

THE MOST DISTURBING BOOK THAT I HAVE EVER READ.
I CANNOT RECOMMEND IT HIGHLY ENOUGH.
ROSARIA BUTTERFIELD
THE
CREAKING
ON THE
STAIRS
FINDING FAITH IN GOD
THROUGH CHILDHOOD ABUSE
MEZ McCONNELL

The Creaking on the Stairs

Finding Faith in God Through Childhood Abuse

Mez McConnell

> I think there is real hope to be found, in the middle of our deepest traumas, in the good news about Jesus Christ. I also think that there is a place for us to find hope and community within the church. Because of these two beliefs, I truly think, distant though it may be, that we may even get to a place of peace within our souls and a place of forgiveness for those who hurt us so much.

This is a book that has no easy answers and will offer none. This is a book that tries to get behind the tough questions of why God permits such abuses to occur in this world. Using his own story of childhood abuse, Mez McConnell tells us about a God who is just, sovereign and loving. A good father who knows the pain of rejection and abuse, who hates evil, who can bring hope even in the darkest place.

This is the most disturbing book that I have ever read, and I cannot recommend it highly enough.

Rosaria Butterfield
Author and speaker

UPDATED EDITION
IS THERE ANYBODY OUT THERE?
A JOURNEY FROM DESPAIR TO HOPE
MEZ McCONNELL
EDITED BY IRENE HOWAT

Is There Anybody Out There?

A Journey from Despair to Hope

Mez McConnell

Since the publication of 'A child called "it"' by Dave Pelzer there hasn't been a story like this. But this is not just another harrowing story about an excruciating childhood and the ravages on a life it produces. The difference is that Mez not only escaped from his 'trial by parent' but he discovered a hope that has transformed his life. He in turn has helped others find hope in their lives. Mez's story is told with a frankness and wit that hides much of the pain and despair that was his everyday experience. Do you like happy endings? Mez still suffers from his experiences but you'll be amazed at how far you can be restored from such a beginning.

This is a compelling, gripping, heart-wrenching, you-can't-put-it-down story of sin and grace. Read this and thank God that, as Psalm 136 says, 'His love endures forever.'

Mark Dever

Senior Pastor, Capitol Hill Baptist Church

FIRST STEPS
SERIES EDITED BY
MEZ McCONNELL
BELIEVE MIKE MCKINLEY
BIBLE ANDREW MATHIESON
CHARACTER SHARON DICKENS
CHURCH J. GARRETT KELL
GOD MEZ McCONNELL
RELATIONSHIPS SHARON DICKENS
SERVICE MEZ McCONNELL
TRAINING ISAAC ADAMS
VOICES ANDY PRIME
WAR MEZ McCONNELL

First Steps Box Set

Edited by Mez McConnell

AN INTERACTIVE GUIDE AND INTRODUCTION TO THE CHRISTIAN LIFE – WARTS AND ALL!

The First Steps series provides an innovative and engaging guide to the Christian Life for people who are just starting out on it, perhaps with no Church background or previous information whatsoever. Possibly excited and nervous at the same time. Each of the ten titles uses everyday language to clearly explain some of the key areas people need to grasp, but commonly struggle with. A unique feature is that you are introduced to a person in each book, who we see trying this out in real life situations. You can almost imagine being there with them.

These ten titles can be followed step–by–step as a path, or in the order that seems most relevant to where you are right now. Volumes include:

- God – Is He Out There?
- War – Why Did Life Just Get Harder?
- Voices – Who Am I Listening To?
- Bible – Can We Trust It?
- Believe – What Should I Know?
- Character – How Do I Change?
- Training – How Do I Grow As A Christian?
- Church – Do I Have To Go?
- Relationships – How Do I Make Things Right?
- Service – How Do I Give Back?

also available from Christian Focus ...

A (Female) Student's Guide to Purity in a Porn Saturated Culture

Helen Thorne-Allenson

We live in a world where pornography is easy to access. At the click of a button, it tempts us to use our devices and bodies to get a cheap hit of excitement, devoid of any real human interaction or care.

But God calls us to a life which is the opposite of that.

Helen Thorne–Allenson shares not only a convincing explanation as to why looking at porn is unhelpful but also some practical tips for breaking the habit.

Christian Focus Publications

Our mission statement

Staying Faithful

In dependence upon God we seek to impact the world through literature faithful to His infallible Word, the Bible. Our aim is to ensure that the Lord Jesus Christ is presented as the only hope to obtain forgiveness of sin, live a useful life and look forward to heaven with Him.

Our Books are published in four imprints:

CHRISTIAN FOCUS

Popular works including biographies, commentaries, basic doctrine and Christian living.

MENTOR

Books written at a level suitable for Bible College and seminary students, pastors, and other serious readers. The imprint includes commentaries, doctrinal studies, examination of current issues and church history.

CHRISTIAN HERITAGE

Books representing some of the best material from the rich heritage of the church.

CF4KIDS

Children's books for quality Bible teaching and for all age groups: Sunday school curriculum, puzzle and activity books; personal and family devotional titles, biographies and inspirational stories – because you are never too young to know Jesus!

Christian Focus Publications Ltd,
Geanies House, Fearn, Ross-shire,
IV20 1TW, Scotland, United Kingdom.
www.christianfocus.com